I DEDICATE THIS BOOK TO MY HUSBAND.

EDITED BY IWONA KIELBUS

BOOK DESIGN BY KATARZYNA BLOCHOWIAK

COPYRIGHT©2025 KATARZYNA BLOCHOWIAK

MY STORY

At the beginning of this book, I would like to share my story with you. As a young person, I suffered from acne, which negatively affected the quality of my life. For many months, I was treated with antibiotics, which brought some improvement to the condition of my skin, but in return had a negative impact on my intestinal microbiome and weakened my digestive system as well as impaired my immunity.

Today, I help people struggling with acne and use novel methods of therapy, such as probiotics and natural products. In my approach to skin diseases and other chronic ailments, I focus on finding the primary causes of the disease, such as disturbed bacterial balance, vitamin and mineral deficiencies, or excess toxins in the body.

I am a **Certified Functional Medicine Practitioner** and a certified nutritionist who graduated from FUNCTIONAL MEDICINE UNIVERSITY in the United States and completed a few other courses in nutrition.

WHAT IS FUNCTIONAL MEDICINE?

Functional Medicine is a science-based approach that focuses on identifying and addressing the root cause of disease. Functional Medicine practitioners look for the physiological and biochemical underlying abnormalities that may be responsible for your disease. They check if any environmental or microbial pathogens have caused the body to be weak and succumb to the disease. Fixing or improving these underlying physiological and biochemical abnormalities leads to a full recovery or at least a long-term reduction of symptoms.

I am also the author of publications for a health magazine "DietPoint" and a speaker at **various** webinars.

Disclaimer of Medical Advice

All readers of this e-book are responsible for their own medical care, treatment, and oversight. All of the content provided in this e-book, including text, advice, dosages, photographs and images are for informational purposes only and do not constitute the providing of medical advice as well as they are not intended to be a substitute for professional medical advice, diagnosis, or treatment.

You should always seek the advice of your qualified health provider with any concerns regarding your health. You should never disregard seeking medical advice relating to your treatment because of the information contained in this e-book.

Copyright©2025 Katarzyna Blochowiak This book is registered with **Protect My Work**

Rights Reserved Notice

Copyright©2025 Katarzyna Blochowiak

All rights reserved. No parts of this e-book may be reproduced without the written permission of the Publisher. For more information, contact the Publisher at **contact@diet-designer.com**.

TABLE OF CONTENTS

The last word to acne

1. PROLOGUE 8

2. DEFINITION OF ACNE 12

   2. SUMMARY 15

3. TYPES OF ACNE 16

   3. SUMMARY 18

4. THE ROLE OF THE SKIN MICROBIOME 19

   4. SUMMARY 23

5. BACTERIA ASSOCIATED WITH ACNE 25

   5. SUMMARY 27

6. GUT-SKIN AXIS IN SKIN DISORDERS 28

   6. SUMMARY 31

7. ORAL MICROBIOME 32

   7. SUMMARY 35

8. HOW TO RESTORE THE SKIN MICROBIOME 36

   8.1. TOPICAL PROBIOTICS 38

   8.1. SUMMARY 40

   8.2. ORAL PROBIOTICS BENEFICIAL FOR SKIN 41

   8.2. SUMMARY 44

9. HOW TO RESTORE THE GUT MICROBIOME 45

   9.1. INTRODUCTION 46

   9.1. SUMMARY 47

   9.2. TIPS TO IMPROVE GUT HEALTH 48

   9.2. SUMMARY 64

10. HOW TO RESTORE ORAL MICROBIOME 67

TABLE OF CONTENTS

The last word to acne

10. SUMMARY 71

11. ACNE AND DIET 72

    11.1. FIVE MAJOR FOOD CLASSES AND FACTORS THAT
PROMOTE ACNE 73

    11.1. SUMMARY 83

    11.2. NUTRITIONAL THERAPY OF ACNE 86

    11.2. SUMMARY 92

12. HORMONES AND ACNE 94

    12. SUMMARY 98

13. HEAVY METALS AND ACNE 99

    13. SUMMARY 101

14. SUPPLEMENTS FOR HEALTHY SKIN 102

    14. SUMMARY 112

15. NATURAL COSMETICS FOR ACNE 114

    15. SUMMARY 122

16. ALTERNATIVE ACNE THERAPIES 123

    16.1. LIGHT THERAPY (PHOTOTHERAPY) 124

    16.2. PHOTOPNEUMATIC THERAPY 125

    16.3. EXFOLIATING FACIAL TREATMENTS 126

    16. SUMMARY 128

17. ACNE DIAGNOSTICS 130

18. EPILOGUE 132

BIBLIOGRAPHY 134

CHAPTER ONE

PROLOGUE

Love your skin again.

Acne vulgaris is a chronic skin disorder that affects almost 80% of teenagers and young adults, often involving psychological and emotional well-being, leading to a reduction in quality of life and sometimes even social isolation. This skin condition often has serious psychological consequences and may lead to low self-esteem and depression, as severe acne can leave disfiguring scars on the face.
Conventional oral and topical treatments available for acne symptoms, leave many patients dissatisfied with their results or experiencing the side effects of those treatments, especially antibiotics therapy.

Do you want to say THE LAST WORD TO ACNE? Do you wish to love your skin again? Are you looking for an effective treatment that will leave your skin looking smooth and healthy? Where is the hidden key to solving your problem?

The answer is to find the root cause of your skin disorder. "THE LAST WORD TO ACNE " gives you exact guidelines on detecting and eliminating the cause of acne symptoms, improving your emotional well-being and overall health. It is a unique comprehensive publication, based on over 60 of the latest scientific studies.

Did you know, for example, that three types of microbiome are involved in acne development? Skin microbiome, oral microbiome, and gut microbiome affect your skin condition. Simple steps, like taking oral probiotics and using topical probiotics can improve your acne symptoms. There are also natural plants and herbs, vitamins, and minerals that can fight acne, both used as supplements or topically. Other available therapies include light therapy and laser therapy.

There is an interesting fact, that populations exposed to a paleolithic diet (low glycemic load, no milk and dairy consumption, natural food) such as the Ache hunters in Paraguay, the Inuit, the Kitavan islanders of Papua New Guinea, and adolescents of rural areas of Brazil are examples of **acne-free populations**. An increase in acne prevalence has been reported for Okinawa islanders, Inuits, and Chinese after the transition from their traditional diets to Western diets. More and more clinical, epidemiological, and translational evidence emphasizes the impact of nutritional factors in the development of acne vulgaris.

The skin is the human body's largest organ that does not exist in isolation from the rest of the body. All substances, and molecules that build our skin cells come from inside, from food we consume. If there is an inflammation inside our body it can affect our skin too.

Nutrients are the building blocks of our cells, internal organs, and skin. They are also a source of energy, and they give our body instructions on how to function. In this sense, **food can be seen as a source of "information" for the body**. I will explain this in more detail.

Cells communicate with each other in a complex language of chemical messages. They instruct each other on how to grow, move, and respond to threats. Problems in cell communication lead to diseases such as acne or diabetes. "Messages" come in many forms, including hormones and charged particles called ions.

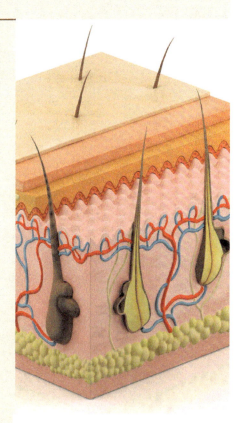

The skin is the human body's largest organ.

Food can be seen as a source of "information" for the body

Copyright©2025 Katarzyna Blochowiak This book is registered with Protect

Recent discoveries show that molecules found in food can alter cellular communication. For example, in 2010, a team of scientists from California and Japan discovered that omega-3 fatty acids from food bind to **specialised** proteins on the surface of cells. This protein, called GPR120, is found in fat and muscle tissue. When an omega-3 fatty acid attaches to the protein, fitting like a key into a lock, it triggers a chain reaction of cellular events that protect the body against inflammation. This is why we can treat food as a source of information for cells that regulate inflammatory response.

You can find a lot of information in this e-book, on how to fight your acne and have a more joyful, better quality life!

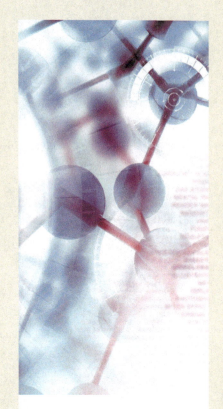

Recent discoveries show that molecules found in food can alter cellular communication.

INSTRUCTION HOW TO READ THIS e-book

If you are very busy or not interested in scientific details you can mainly focus on summaries of each chapter (green pages). Summaries will also help you to better memorise the most important information.
I invite you to join our journey to feel comfortable in your own skin and love your skin again!

CHAPTER TWO

DEFINITION OF ACNE

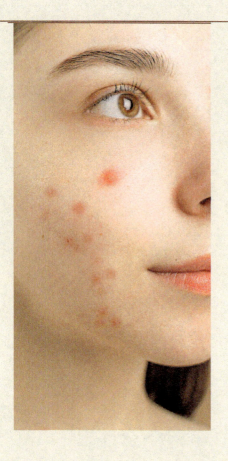

Acne vulgaris is a common skin condition characterized by red pimples on the skin, especially on the face. Inflamed or infected sebaceous glands are causing acne, mainly among adolescents but many adults are also affected.

In this condition sebum—oil that prevents skin from drying out—and dead skin cells plug the pores. It could lead to outbreaks of lesions, commonly called pimples. In most cases, the outbreaks occur on the face but can also appear on the chest, back, or shoulders.

The sebaceous glands in healthy skin make sebum that empties onto the skin surface through the pore, which is an opening in the follicle. The follicle is lined with keratinocytes which is a type of skin cell. In healthy skin, as the body sheds skin cells, the keratinocytes rise to the surface of the skin. In the case of acne, sebum, and keratinocytes stick together inside the pore. This enables the shedding of the keratinocytes and keeps the sebum from reaching the surface of the skin.

The mixture of oil and keratinocytes in the plugged follicles causes the growth of the bacteria that normally live on the skin surface. It leads to inflammation—swelling, redness, and pain.

The wall of the plugged follicle finally breaks down and spills sebum, skin cells, and the bacteria, into nearby skin, creating pimples or lesions.

Many factors contribute to the development of acne, including:

- hormonal changes
- diet
- infections
- genetics
- stress

The pathogenesis (the process by which a disorder develops) of acne is multifactorial, including genetic and metabolic factors, and hormonal changes, in which both gut and skin microbiota are involved. Many studies show the bidirectionality between the intestinal microbiota and skin homeostasis (balance) because the gut microbiome modifies the immune system response, which affects also skin immunity and skin condition.

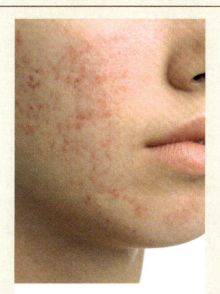

Four major causes have been identified by scientists as primary influences on acne occurrence:

1) increased sebum production and modification of its composition

2) hyperkeratinization (cells of the follicle become cohesive and do not shed normally onto the skin's surface)

3) abnormal microbial flora, particularly colonization by Cutibacterium acnes (formerly Propionibacterium acnes), Staphylococcus aureus, Staphylococcus epidermidis

4) inflammation

Four major causes as primary influences on acne occurrence:

1) increased sebum production and modification of its composition

2) hyperkeratinization

3) abnormal microbial flora

4) inflammation

CHAPTER TWO SUMMARY

DEFINITION OF ACNE

Acne vulgaris is a common skin condition characterized by red pimples on the skin, especially on the face.
In this condition sebum—oil that prevents skin from drying out—and dead skin cells plug the pores. The mixture of oil and keratinocytes in the plugged follicles causes the growth of the bacteria that normally live on the skin surface. It leads to inflammation—swelling, redness and pain.

Four major causes that influence on acne occurrence:

1) increased sebum production and modification of its composition

2) **hyperkeratinization** (cells of the follicle become cohesive and do not shed normally onto the skin's surface)

3) **abnormal microbial flora**, particularly colonization by **Cutibacterium acnes** (formerly Propionibacterium acnes), Staphylococcus aureus, Staphylococcus epidermidis

4) **inflammation**

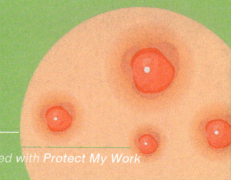

CHAPTER THREE

TYPES OF ACNE

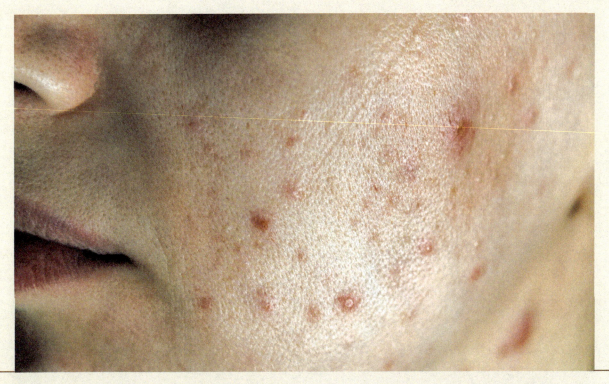

Acne causes a few types of pimples or lesions.

TYPES OF ACNE INCLUDE:

- **Whiteheads**

Whiteheads are defined as plugged hair follicles beneath the skin. They produce a white bump.

- **Blackheads**

Blackheads are defined as plugged follicles that reach the surface of the skin and open up. Blackheads have a black color because the air discolors the sebum, not because they are dirty.

- **Pustules or pimples**

Pustules or pimples are topped by yellow pus-filled lesions that can be red at the base.

- **Papules**

Papules are defined as inflamed lesions that look like small, pink bumps on the skin and can be tender to the touch.

- **Nodules**

Nodules are defined as large, painful lesions that are located deep within the skin.

- **Severe nodular acne (called also cystic acne)**

Severe nodular acne is defined as deep, painful, and filled with pus lesions.

CHAPTER THREE SUMMARY

TYPES OF ACNE

Types of acne include:

- Whiteheads
- Blackheads
- Pustules or pimples
- Papules
- Nodules
- Severe nodular acne (called also cystic acne)

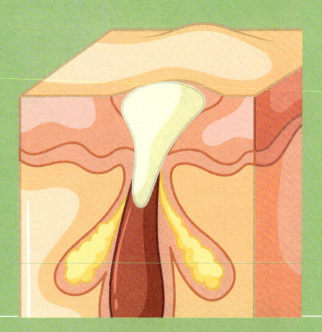

CHAPTER FOUR

THE ROLE OF THE SKIN MICROBIOME

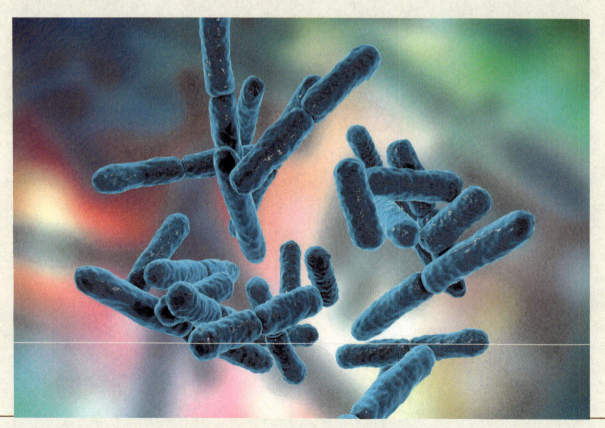

Did you know that three types of microbiome affect your skin health?

These are the skin microbiome, oral microbiome and gut microbiome.

Have you ever heard that skin is home to our friendly health-promoting bacteria and fungi?

Many people think that bacteria and other microorganisms are harmful "germs" and are our enemies but actually, many bacteria and yeast are our friends fighting pathogens and producing many substances that are beneficial for our health.
The microbiome is a scientific term that refers to the collection of all microbes, such as bacteria, viruses, fungi, and their genes, that live on our bodies and inside us.
The skin is the human body's largest organ, colonized by millions of diverse microorganisms, including:

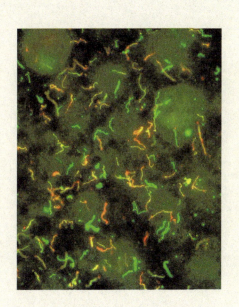

- **bacteria** - Staphylococcus, Corynebacterium, Enhydrobacter, Micrococcus, Cutibacterium, Brevibacterium, Dermabacter, Veillonella, Roseomonas mucosa, Pseudomonas, Actinetobacter, Pantoea septica, Moraxella osloensis

- **archaea** (single-celled microorganisms with structure similar to bacteria) - Thaumarchaeota, Euryarchaeota

- **fungi** - Malassezia, Cryptococcus, Candida, Rhodotorula.

Cutibacterium and Malassezia dominate in the sebaceous areas of the skin.

The quantity and diversity of skin microorganisms depend on factors such as the amount of sebum, skin hydration, pH, and UV radiation.

Many microbes populating the skin can produce molecules that inhibit the colonisation of other microorganisms, for example, pathogenic bacteria.

Skin microorganisms communicate with immune system cells, triggering a local and global immune response. This is a bidirectional communication involving various messengers, e.g. immune system cells, hormones, pro-inflammatory and anti-inflammatory cytokines, and bacterial metabolites (substances produced by bacteria). Cytokines are proteins that help control inflammation in your body.
Skin microbiome plays an important role in shaping the response of the skin's immune system.

The imbalance in the skin microbiome causes a whole range of inflammation, inducing conditions such as acne, atopic dermatitis, psoriasis, rosacea, dandruff, and seborrheic dermatitis.

Probiotic bacteria are essential for our health. The skin microbiome includes many species of microorganisms. Any imbalance in the microbiome can cause skin disorders.

Every person's microbiome is unique. There are also various strains of microorganisms depending on the part of the body where the microbes were collected.

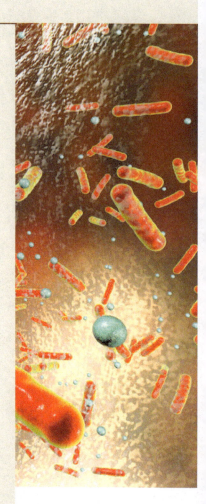

An imbalance in the skin microbiome causes acne, atopic dermatitis, psoriasis, rosacea, dandruff, and seborrheic dermatitis.

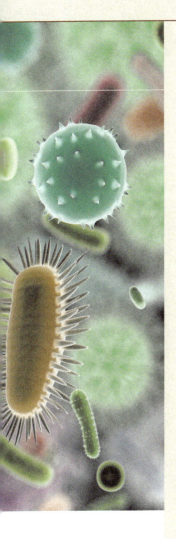

Gut microbiome is different from the skin microbiome.

The skin microbiome has many functions, including defence against pathogens and boosting the skin's immune function. The skin bacteria are also involved in wound healing.

Certain strains of bacteria also produce some products that increase our immunity thanks to antimicrobial, anti-inflammatory, or anti-neoplastic activity.

Staphylococcus aureus in the skin can convert histidine (an essential amino acid) to another amino acid that further converts to trans urocanic acid. Urocanic acid absorbs and blocks ultraviolet (UV) radiation offering similar skin protection to sunscreens.

Some Staphylococcus species have antibacterial properties protecting your skin from pathogenic bacteria. Staphylococcus epidermidis shows anticancer properties.

The skin microbiome has many functions, including defence against pathogens and boosting the skin's immune function.

CHAPTER FOUR
SUMMARY

THE ROLE OF THE SKIN MICROBIOME

The microbiome is a scientific term that refers to the collection of all microbes, such as bacteria, viruses, fungi, and their genes, that live on our bodies and inside us.

The skin is the human body's largest organ, colonised by millions of diverse microorganisms, including:

• **bacteria** - Staphylococcus, Corynebacterium, Enhydrobacter, Micrococcus, Cutibacterium, Brevibacterium, Dermabacter, Veillonella, Roseomonas mucosa, Pseudomonas, Actinetobacter, Pantoea septica, Moraxella osloensis

• **archaea** - (single-celled microorganisms with structure similar to bacteria)-Thaumarchaeota, Euryarchaeota

• **fungi** - Malassezia, Cryptococcus, Candida, Rhodotorula

Cutibacterium and Malassezia dominate in the sebaceous areas of the skin.

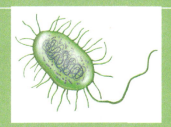

The imbalance in the skin microbiome causes a whole range of inflammation, inducing conditions such as **acne, atopic dermatitis, psoriasis, rosacea, dandruff, and seborrheic dermatitis.**

Gut microbiome is different from the skin microbiome.

There are many functions of the skin microbiome, including defence against pathogens and boosting the skin's immune function. The skin bacteria are also involved in wound healing. Certain strains of them show antimicrobial, anti-inflammatory, or anti-neoplastic activity. Staphylococcus aureus is able to absorb and block ultraviolet (UV) radiation offering similar skin protection to sunscreens. Staphylococcus epidermidis shows anticancer properties.

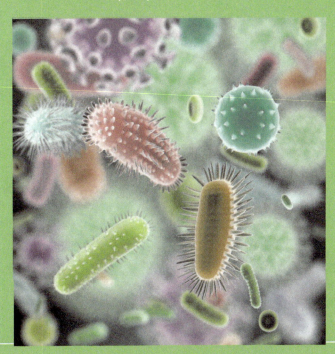

CHAPTER FIVE

BACTERIA ASSOCIATED WITH ACNE

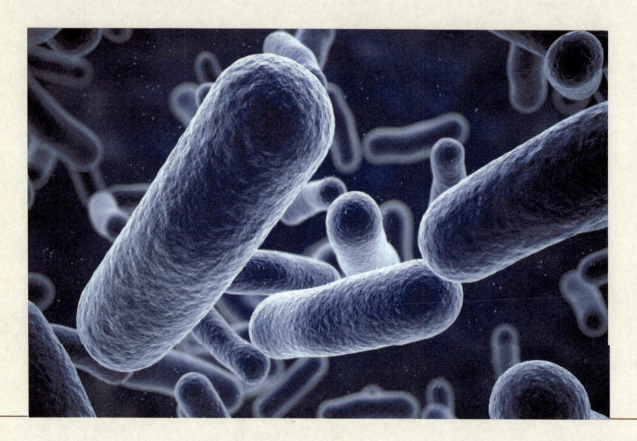

In inflammatory skin diseases, like acne, a reduced number of Bifidobacterium and Lactobacillus is observed.

The primary bacterium associated with acne is Cutibacterium acnes (formerly Propionibacterium acnes). This bacterium colonizes sebaceous follicles and secretes some enzymes like proteases, lipases and hyaluronidases, causing skin inflammation.

Adolescence is a time of hormonal changes, including increased production of **Insulin-like growth factor 1 (IGF-1)**. This hormone causes excessive sebum production which increases colonisation of Cutibacterium acnes.

There are also other bacteria that cause skin inflammation and acne, like **Staphylococcus epidermidis, Streptococcus pneumoniae, Staphylococcus aureus, Klebsiella pneumonia, and Enterobacter.**

An imbalance in the skin microbiome caused by puberty, poor diet, stress, and lifestyle leads to skin inflammation and acne.

Conventional acne treatment includes oral antibiotics and topical antibacterial ointments. The new approach consists of the use of oral and topical probiotics to balance the skin microbiome targeting the root cause of this skin disorder.

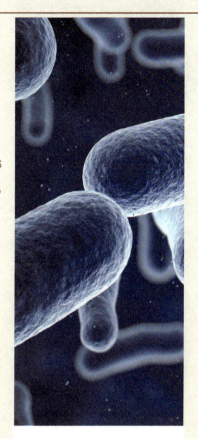

The primary bacterium associated with acne is Cutibacterium acnes.

CHAPTER FIVE SUMMARY

BACTERIA ASSOCIATED WITH ACNE

In inflammatory skin diseases, like acne, a **reduced number of Bifidobacterium and Lactobacillus** is observed.

The primary bacterium associated with acne is Cutibacterium acnes (formerly Propionibacterium acnes). This bacterium colonizes sebaceous follicles, causing skin inflammation.

There are also other bacteria that cause acne, like **Staphylococcus epidermidis, Streptococcus pneumoniae, Staphylococcus aureus, Klebsiella pneumoniae and Enterobacter.**

The new approach to acne treatment includes the use of oral and topical probiotics to balance the skin microbiome targeting the root cause of this skin disorder.

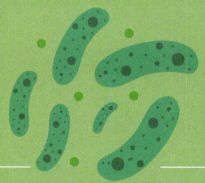

CHAPTER SIX

GUT-SKIN AXIS IN SKIN DISORDERS

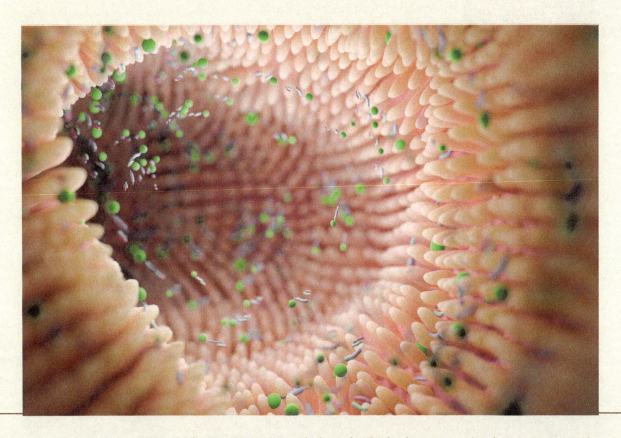

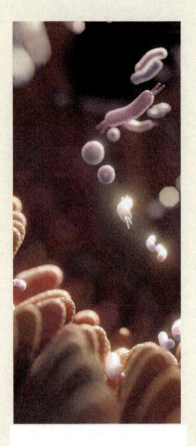

Many studies show the connection between inflammatory skin conditions and the imbalanced gut microbiome.

First of all the gut microbiome influences the immune system. The role of the immune system is to protect us against pathogens. Dysbiosis (an imbalance in bacterial composition) in the gut microflora may lead to inflammation not only in the gut but also in other organs such as the skin, leading to acne, atopic dermatitis, psoriasis, or rosacea.

Scientific evidence shows that the interaction between the microorganisms and the host immune system is essential to maintain skin homeostasis (skin balance). Therefore logical approach leads us to the conclusion that balancing the skin microbiome and gut microbiome is a good idea in treating skin conditions.

High quality multi-strain probiotics play a key role in restoring the microbiome and treating many inflammatory skin diseases.

The intestinal microbiome is involved in the formation of acne lesions. The quality of the microbiome inhabiting the intestines affects both gut and skin conditions. An increasing number of studies indicate that the health of the gut is related to the health of the skin. Research on the microbiome has to be continued, as the connection between gut and skin conditions has not been fully investigated.

Many studies show the connection between inflammatory skin conditions and the imbalanced gut microbiome.

The Western diet, which primarily consists of processed foods, soft drinks, and fast food, disturbs the balance between beneficial and pathogenic microorganisms, which leads to inflammation, including **inflammatory skin disorders like acne.**

Stress also affects the microbiome, and beneficial bacteria Lactobacillus and Bifidobacterium are very sensitive to its effects. Under stress, microorganisms produce some neurotransmitters that are inflammatory to the body.

The intestinal microbiome can also modify the production of **short-chain fatty acids (SCFAs).** SCFAs are very important for our health because they nourish intestinal cells and modulate brain activity. One example is propionic acid, which is toxic to Staphylococcus aureus. SCFAs may also improve skin's resistance to cutaneous Staphylococcus and Cutibacterium acnes.

CHAPTER SIX
SUMMARY

GUT-SKIN AXIS IN SKIN DISORDERS

Many studies show the connection between inflammatory skin conditions and the imbalanced gut microbiome.

First of all the gut microbiome influences the immune system. The role of the immune system is to protect us against pathogens. Dysbiosis (an imbalance in bacterial composition) in the gut microflora may lead to inflammation not only in the gut but also in other organs such as the skin, leading to acne, atopic dermatitis, psoriasis, or rosacea.

High quality multi-strain probiotics play a key role in restoring the microbiome and treating many inflammatory skin diseases.

The intestinal microbiome can also modify the production of short-chain fatty acids (SCFAs) which are very important for our health because they nourish intestinal cells and modulate brain activity. One example is propionic acid, which is toxic to Staphylococcus aureus. SCFAs may also improve skin's resistance to cutaneous Staphylococcus and Cutibacterium acnes.

CHAPTER SEVEN

ORAL MICROBIOME

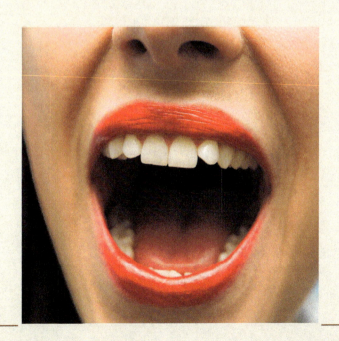

Many scientific studies have shown connections between oral health, the presence of specific bacterial species, and a variety of autoimmune skin conditions, indicating that oral microbiome could be a modifiable risk factor for these skin disorders.

The oral microbiome is very important for intestinal health too because we can get translocation of pathogens from the mouth to the gut and that can cause GI dysbiosis and change immune defense as well.

In the mouth, we have bacteria, archaea (single-celled microorganisms with structure similar to bacteria), viruses, fungi, and protozoans. We can find more than 700 species of bacteria in the mouth.

The microbiome shifts between different body sites. The oral and the gastrointestinal microflora shows the greatest diversity and both are linked to one another.

Many bacterial species in the oral microbiome are associated with health and healthy skin, including several species of Streptococci, like Streptococcus salivarius, S. mitis, S. oralis, and S. sanguinis as well as bacteria from the Veillonella and Actinomyces genuses.

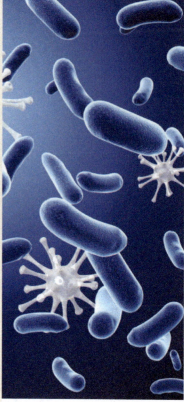

In the mouth, we have bacteria, archaea, viruses, fungi, and protozoans.

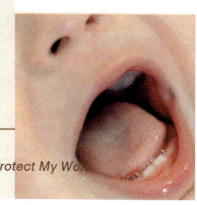

Copyright©2025 Katarzyna Blochowiak This book is registered with **Protect My Wo**

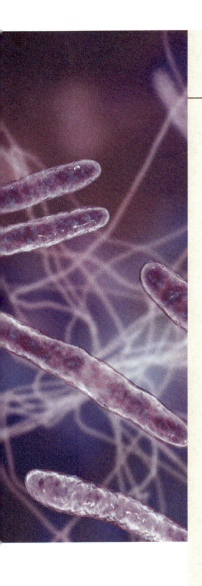

On the other hand, the presence of dysbiotic species, like Acholeplasma, Fretibacterium, Porphyromonas gingivalis, Peptococcus, Treponem denticola, Defluviitaleaceae, Filifactor, and Mycoplasma were associated with periodontal disease and skin disorders.

Periodontal disease and dysbiotic bacteria appear to play a role in many dermatologic diseases.

More than 500 species of microorganisms have been isolated from periodontal disease patients. Those oral microorganisms can reach the heart, lungs, and peripheral blood capillary system, affecting our overall health.

Periodontal disease and dysbiotic bacteria appear to play a role in many dermatologic diseases.

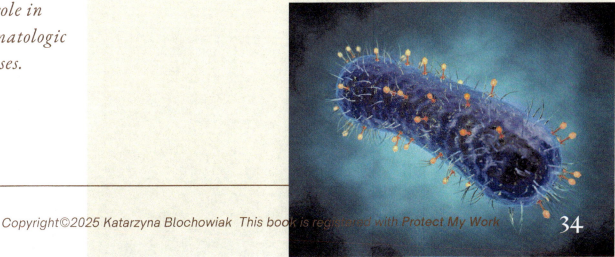

CHAPTER SEVEN SUMMARY

ORAL MICROBIOME

There are connections between oral health, the presence of specific bacterial species and a variety of autoimmune skin conditions indicating that oral microbiome could be a modifiable risk factor for skin disorders.

In the mouth, we have bacteria, archaea, viruses, fungi, and protozoans. We can find more than 700 species of bacteria in the mouth.

The presence of dysbiotic species, like Acholeplasma, Fretibacterium, Porphyromonas gingivalis, Peptococcus, Treponem denticola, Defluviitaleaceae, Filifactor, and Mycoplasma is associated with skin disorders and periodontal disease. On the other hand, many bacterial species in the oral microbiome are associated with health and healthy skin, like Streptococcus salivarius, S. mitis, S. oralis, and S. sanguinis as well as bacteria from the Veillonella and Actinomyces genuses.

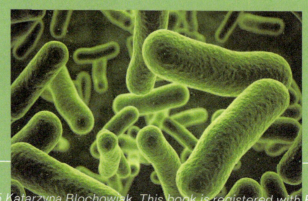

CHAPTER EIGHT

HOW TO RESTORE THE SKIN MICROBIOME

A new therapeutic approach in treating skin diseases includes using topical and oral probiotics.

Probiotics can restore skin balance and promote self-healing.

Probiotics are live microorganisms including bacteria and/or yeast that live in your body. Probiotics are basically good bacteria that maintain human health and prevent us from diseases.

Some good bacteria destroy disease-causing cells or pathogenic bacteria, others help digest food or even produce vitamins.

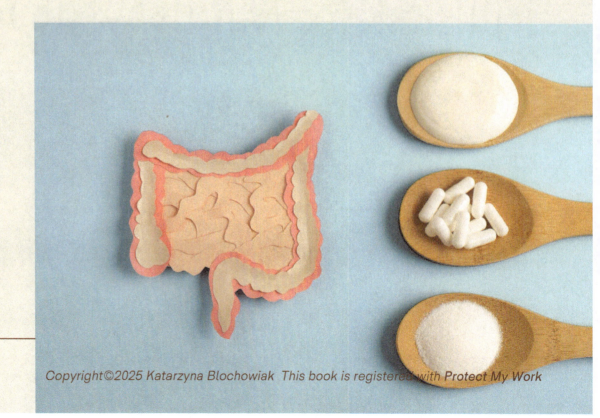

8.1. TOPICAL PROBIOTICS

Scientific evidence shows that topical probiotics could have beneficial effects for the treatment of many skin diseases such as acne, psoriasis, rosacea, and others. They are also effective in wound healing. Topical probiotics available on the market include sprays, lotions, creams, cleansers and masks.

Probiotic-impregnated fabrics are also a new ingenious solution in fighting skin disorders.

Beneficial bacteria can produce certain antimicrobial amino peptides which enhance the skin's immune responses and are involved in pathogens' elimination. The topical application of probiotic bacteria helps to protect the skin's natural barrier.

For example, bacterium Streptococcus thermophiles enhances ceramide production when applied as a cream. By producing ceramides, probiotics help strengthen the skin barrier and soothe irritated skin. Ceramides are fats or lipids that are found in skin cells. They help to moisturise and strengthen the protective skin moisture barrier. Certain ceramide sphingolipids such as Phytosphingosine show antimicrobial activity against Cutibacterium acnes, improving acne. Phytosphingosine is a complex fatty alcohol that occurs naturally in the skin's upper layers. Its role is to maintain the skin's natural moisturising factor for healthy condition. Other studies show that application of phytosphingosine reduces pustules and papules in patients with acne.

Scientific evidence shows that topical probiotics could have beneficial effects for the treatment of many skin diseases such as acne, psoriasis, rosacea, and others.

Scientists discovered also that Enterococcus faecalis SL-5 applied topically as a lotion significantly reduced pustules. Enterococcus faecalis SL-5 demonstrates anti-Cutibacterium acnes activity.

An extract of Lactobacillus plantarum also reduced acne severity (i.e., acne size, count, and erythema).

There is also one study showing that Streptococcus salivarius, an important strain found in healthy humans' oral microbiome, inhibits Cutibacterium acnes. Other studies demonstrate that the bad bacteria, which resides in an infected tooth or gum can infect the face as well and result in a acne in the skin.

Scientific evidences above show a potential role of topical probiotics in the treatment of acne and could be possibly used as an alternative to topical antibiotics.

Novel approach indicates that topical probiotics can act as protective barrier, reduce the pustules, fight acne-causing bacteria and reduce skin irritation in acne patients.

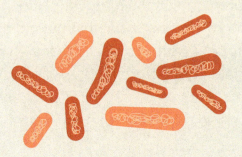

Novel approach shows that topical probiotics can act as protective barrier, reduce the pustules, fight acne-causing bacteria and reduce skin irritation in acne patients.

CHAPTER EIGHT SUMMARY

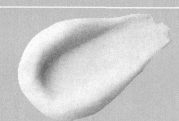

8.1. TOPICAL PROBIOTICS

A new therapeutic approach in treating skin diseases includes using topical and oral probiotics. Probiotics can restore skin balance and promote self-healing.

This novel approach shows that topical probiotics can act as a protective barrier, reduce the pustules, fight acne-causing bacteria and reduce skin irritation in acne patients.

Scientific evidence indicates that topical probiotics could have beneficial effects for the treatment of many skin diseases such as acne, psoriasis, rosacea and others. They are also effective in wound healing.

Topical probiotics available on the market include sprays, lotions, creams, cleansers and masks. Probiotic-impregnated fabrics are also a new ingenious solution in fighting skin disorders.

For example, Enterococcus faecalis SL-5 applied topically as a lotion significantly reduced pustules and demonstrates anti-Cutibacterium acnes activity. An extract of Lactobacillus plantarum also reduced acne severity (i.e., acne size, count, and erythema). Streptococcus salivarius inhibits Cutibacterium acnes as well. Streptococcus thermophiles enhances ceramide production when applied as a cream. Ceramides play a key role in structuring and maintaining the water permeability barrier function of the skin.

8.2. ORAL PROBIOTICS BENEFICIAL FOR SKIN

Scientific evidence shows that oral probiotics can help in improving immune reactions beyond the gut and expand them towards the skin in people suffering from acne. Oral supplementation of certain probiotics is especially beneficial for skin health.

Scientists also found the symbiotic ability of probiotic bacteria and dietary fiber (prebiotic) konjac glucomannan hydrolysates to inhibit Cutibacterium acnes growth.

Below is a list of probiotics that can help fight acne. There are many multi-strain probiotics available on the market, so you do not have to buy most of them as a single strain.

Lactobacillus
Skin benefits:

The most common cause of adult acne is the overproduction of sebum (a type of oil secreted by our skin) and the presence of certain bacteria strains beneath the skin. Lactobacillus has been proven to improve acne by fighting the bacteria beneath the skin and reducing sebum production. There are skin care products available, like cleansers or masks containing those strains of bacteria. Lactobacillus produces natural enzymes that help break down the sebum, which makes the skin less oily and improves its function and opens clogged pores.

Lactobacillus paracasei NCC2461 (or ST11) has been shown to reduce inflammation in the skin.

Scientific evidence shows that oral probiotics can help in improving immune reactions beyond the gut and expand them towards the skin in people suffering from acne.

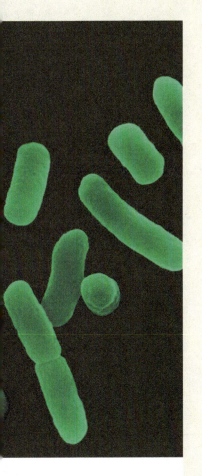

Bifidobacterium
Skin benefits:

In inflammatory skin diseases, a reduced number of Bifidobacterium is observed.

Lactobacilli and Bifidobacteria decrease inflammation and acne is an inflammatory condition. Scientific evidence shows that those strains reduce the release of pro-inflammatory cytokines (TNF-α, IL-6, and IL-8) and increase the release of anti-inflammatory cytokines (IL-10). Cytokine is a type of protein that has an effect on the immune system.

Bifidobacterium infantis 35624 is especially recommended for acne patients and for skin disorders. This strain has a beneficial effect on the gut microbiome and intestinal functioning. It calms down inflammation and repairs your gut lining thanks to the production of butyric acid.

Bacillus
Skin benefits:

Bacillus Coagulans is able to modulate the activity of the immune system and reduce damage by reactive oxygen species (ROS). ROS are substances that cause damage to the skin and promote inflammation and aging.

Streptococcus salivarius

Skin benefits:

Streptococcus salivarius K12 has been shown to inhibit the growth of Cutibacterium acnes and decrease inflammatory markers internally that are associated with acne.

Saccharomyces Boulardii

Skin benefits:

Saccharomyces Boulardii is a beneficial type of yeast that is helpful in healing acne and balancing the microbiome.

Enterococcus faecalis

Skin benefits:

An increasing concern in acne treatment is antibiotic-resistant Cutibacterium acnes and dysbiosis of the skin microbiome. Probiotic Enterococcus faecalis shows benefits for acne treatment by exerting antimicrobial activity against Cutibacterium acnes.

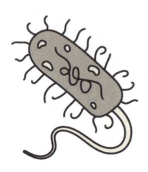

Akkermansia muciniphila

Skin benefits:

Some dermatologists are using Akkermansia muciniphila with their patients to fight acne, rosacea, and atopic dermatitis.

CHAPTER EIGHT SUMMARY

8.2. ORAL PROBIOTICS BENEFICIAL FOR SKIN

Scientific evidence shows that oral probiotics can help in improving immune reactions beyond the gut and expand them towards the skin in people suffering from acne.

Below is a list of probiotics that can help fight acne. There are many multi-strain probiotics available on the market, so you do not have to buy most of them as a single strain.

Lactobacillus, especially Lactobacillus paracasei NCC2461
Bifidobacterium, especially Bifidobacterium infantis 35624
Bacillus
Streptococcus salivarius
Saccharomyces Boulardii
Enterococcus faecalis
Akkermansia muciniphila

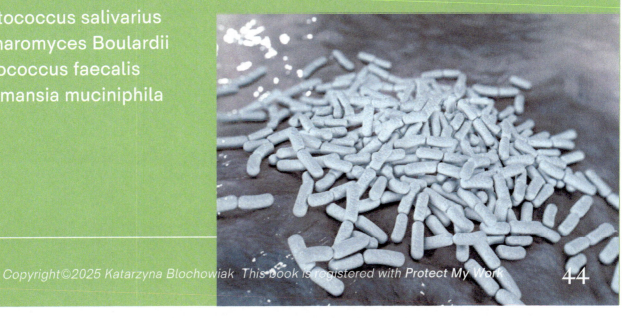

CHAPTER NINE

HOW TO RESTORE THE GUT MICROBIOME

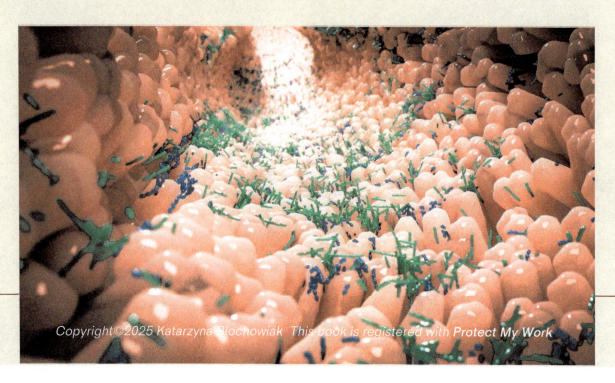

9.1. INTRODUCTION

As mentioned before, scientists discovered a link between the imbalanced gut and inflammatory skin diseases.

This means that gut healing using probiotics and other supplements should also be considered as a treatment option for skin disorders.

Growing evidence shows that probiotics modify the factors that contribute to acne. They can inhibit Cutibacterium acnes with antimicrobial proteins.

Probiotics also show immunomodulatory properties on keratinocytes. Keratinocytes are the most dominant cell type constituting the epidermis and play an essential role in skin repair.

For example Lactobacillus paracasei NCC2461 can suppress substance P-induced skin inflammation. Substance P is involved in sebum production and acne inflammation.

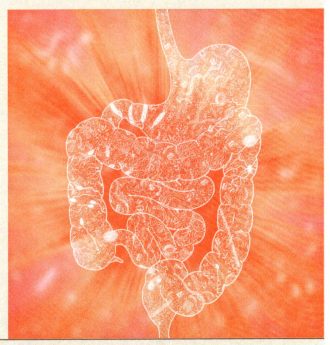

CHAPTER NINE SUMMARY

9.1. INTRODUCTION

As mentioned before scientists discovered a link between the imbalanced gut and inflammatory skin diseases.

This means that gut healing using probiotics and other supplements should also be considered as a treatment option for skin disorders.

Growing evidence shows that probiotics modify the factors that contribute to acne.

9.2. TIPS TO IMPROVE GUT HEALTH

A scientific study from 2018 has proven that people with acne have completely different gut bacteria and fungus strains compared to those without acne. **The study found that acne correlates with poorer gut diversity. This means that people with skin problems have gut dysbiosis, an imbalance in the intestinal microbiome. The discovery indicates a link between gut health and acne, thus healing your gut will improve your skin condition.**

The recommendation would be to consult a Functional Medicine Practitioner or other IBS practitioner to prepare GUT HEALING PROTOCOL which will be tailored for you and based on diagnostic tests verifying what is the root cause of your gut problems.

Below you can find the GUT HEALING PROGRAMME that explains the whole process of restoring balance in your intestine.

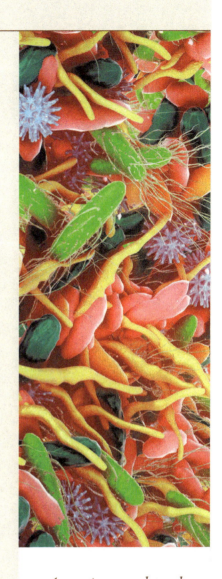

Acne is correlated with less gut diversity. This means that people with skin problems have gut dysbiosis, an imbalance in the intestinal microbiome.

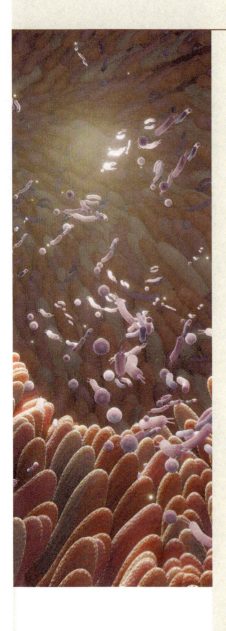

GUT HEALING PROGRAMME

1. IDENTIFY AND REMOVE THE POTENTIAL UNDERLYING CAUSE OF THE GUT IMBALANCE

The first step is to identify and remove the potential underlying cause of the gut imbalance. This relates to inflammatory foods and/or disbiotic/pathogenic microbes in the gut. This stage will reduce inflammation.

Observe your reactions after consuming different types of foods and eliminate for at least 3 months products causing gut symptoms. Elimination diet is the gold standard method of identifying any food intolerance. **Symptoms should fade or disappear when removing the food and return upon reintroducing it.**

Unfortunately, the symptoms can be delayed making identification of problematic food more difficult. In this case, the good idea is to perform a food sensitivities test.

A test used to diagnose food sensitivities and commonly available is the **food IgG test.**
IgG is a type of antibody (antibodies are major components of the immune system) that can be formed when you react to foods. A blood test is used to measure food-specific IgG antibodies to identify foods to which you may be sensitive.

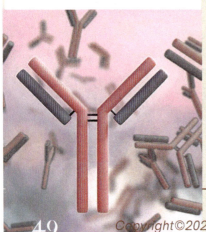

Copyright©2025 Katarzyna Blochowiak This book is registered with **Protect My Work**

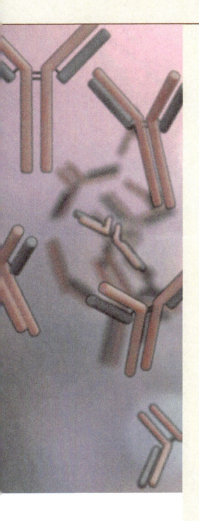

Unfortunately, the IgG test does not detect all types of food sensitivities. There is **cellular test that measures immune cells respond to food products.**

The difference between this test and IgG antibody testing is that it uses the cellular approach, which is more accurate and checks more types of food sensitivity reactions. Multiple pathogenic mechanisms mediate food and chemical sensitivities, not only those involving IgG antibodies. By using the cellular approach, instead of a single antibody such as IgG, this cellular test can identify food and chemical sensitivities regardless of the pathway. The cells can release free radicals and inflammatory mediators without antibody involvement. Cellular test measures the total amount of inflammation caused by food substance, while IgG antibody testing measures antibodies, but not inflammation.

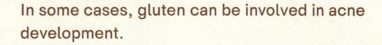

In some cases, gluten can be involved in acne development.

Studies show links between coeliac disease and several skin conditions, including acne, eczema, psoriasis, and urticaria. Coeliac disease increases inflammation in the body and acne is an inflammatory skin condition. If you have any bad reaction after consuming gluten, perform a test for gluten sensitivity and coeliac disease.

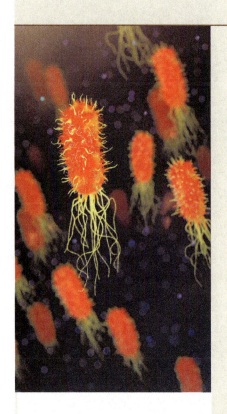

Regarding problematic microbes or pathogens, testing is the best way to identify if gut infection is caused by dysbiotic bacteria, yeasts, or parasites. **The Comprehensive Stool Analysis with Parasitology and PCR** evaluates the status of beneficial bacteria, imbalanced commensal bacteria, disbiotic bacteria, pathogenic bacteria, parasites, and yeasts like Candida.
Removing them using natural anti-microbial supplements or with medication is an important step to reduce inflammation.

At this stage the good idea is to support your immune system with natural supplements, to strengthen your body in advance. Some examples are fish oil, liposomal glutathione, or PEA (Palmitoylethanolamide).

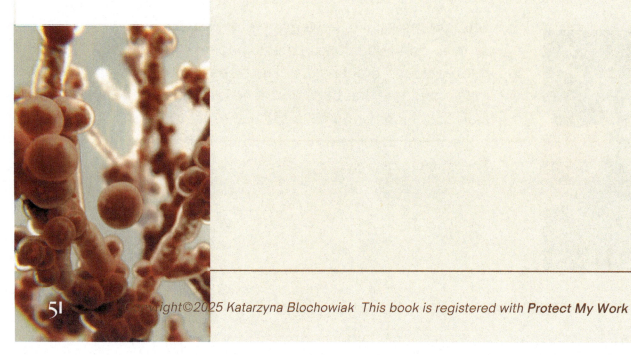

2. INTRODUCE NUTRIENTS AND SUPPLEMENTS THAT SUPPORT THE BREAKDOWN AND ABSORPTION OF FOOD.

Use certain supplements that support the breakdown and absorption of food.

It should be chosen depending on your test results or symptoms. This can be HCl (stomach acid), digestive enzymes, bile support, short-chain fatty acids (like butyrate), or anti-inflammatory supplements. Discuss with a Functional Medicine Practitioner or other IBS practitioner what will work best for you.

Supplementation of certain vitamins and minerals can also be helpful if the tests show that you are deficient, for instance vitamin D, A, or zinc.

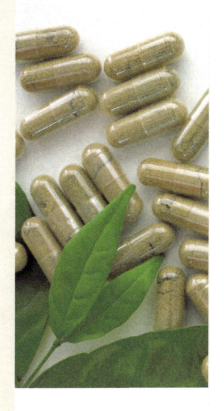

It is also important to support liver function. The liver can affect acne through its role in fat digestion. **Poor liver function can lead to increased fats in your bloodstream, which can stimulate sebum production and clog your pores, causing breakouts and acne. The liver health affects hormonal balance too.** Poor liver function can lead to hormonal acne because it does not regulate hormone levels in the bloodstream effectively. Toxins in the liver can overload this organ, leading to poor liver detoxification. This is another way poor liver function affects skin conditions like acne vulgaris, rosacea, and psoriasis. To support your liver, change your diet and supplement with Milk Thistle or Artichoke Leaf Extract.

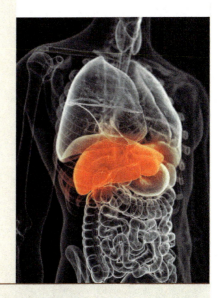

3. REPOPULATE YOUR BENEFICIAL BACTERIA

Repopulate your beneficial bacteria using prebiotic and probiotic-rich foods and good quality muti-strains probiotic supplements. A healthy microbiome provides optimal digestion and normal immune function. Multi-strain probiotics are composed of more than one species of bacteria and often fungal species too. The mechanisms by which multi-strain probiotics work include modulation of the immune system, eradication of pathogens, stimulation of digestive enzymes and interactions with the host tissues. Multi-strain probiotics can help to alleviate many diseases, inhibit pathogens, and restore the gut microbiome.

Below are examples of probiotic strains and their benefits for the gut.

Lactobacillus
Gut benefits:

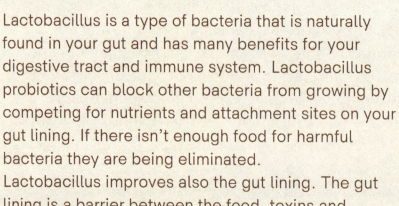

Lactobacillus is a type of bacteria that is naturally found in your gut and has many benefits for your digestive tract and immune system. Lactobacillus probiotics can block other bacteria from growing by competing for nutrients and attachment sites on your gut lining. If there isn't enough food for harmful bacteria they are being eliminated.
Lactobacillus improves also the gut lining. The gut lining is a barrier between the food, toxins and microbes in your intestine and your bloodstream. This lining is made of cells with shared membranes called tight junctions.

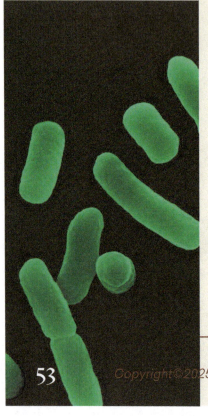

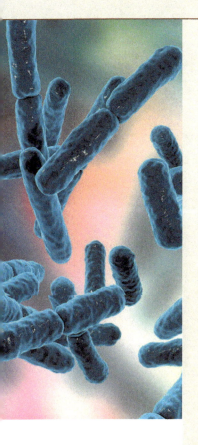

Damage to the gut lining makes the tight junctions loosen, which causes leakage of harmful compounds into your bloodstream. Lactobacillus stimulates different types of reactions in the gut that make these tight junctions work better.

Bifidobacterium
Gut benefits:

Bifidobacteria probiotic supplementation can rebalance the gut microbiome by boosting the levels of beneficial bacteria and inhibiting the growth of more harmful bacteria.

Bacillus
Gut benefits:

Bacillus Coagulans is a unique probiotic strain resistant to gastric acid and heat. These bacteria form reproductive structures called spores. Spore-forming bacteria are protected in a special way because their coating consists of a form of a protein, that allows them to survive in the stomach acid and to reach and colonise the small intestine, where they will germinate and multiply.
Bacillus Coagulans improves the immune system and might treat diarrhoea and constipation.
Contrary to popular belief, the human body can produce its own vitamin C. This is done by a specific species of gut microbes — the bacillus. Bacillus converts sugar into vitamin C. This probiotic is also involved in producing vitamin K.

Contrary to popular belief, the human body can produce its own vitamin C.

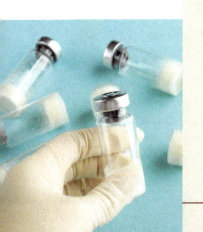

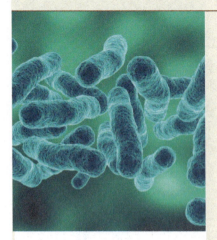

Spore probiotics can reestablish your gut microbiome more effectively because they do not get destroyed by antibiotics.

The bacillus very effectively modulate cytokines — anti-inflammatory cytokines are upregulated while inflammatory cytokines are downregulated, thereby restoring a balance between the two.

Saccharomyces Boulardii
Gut benefits:

Saccharomyces boulardii is not targeted by antibiotics because is yeast-based. This means the S. boulardii probiotic survives the antibiotic treatment and fosters healthy intestinal flora. This probiotic strain also stimulates the production of Immunoglobulin A (IgA) — the main antibody in the gut that helps defend against infections. S. boulardii helps restore the balance of microbiota by flushing out harmful bacteria to make room for good bacteria to flourish. It increases the production of digestive enzymes too, which help break down dietary sugars. This improves the absorption of water and nutrients in your small intestine.

Enterococcus faecalis
Gut benefits:

Enterococcus faecalis is a bacterium that produces vitamins, metabolises nutrients, and maintains intestinal pH. It has a positive impact on the human immune system too.

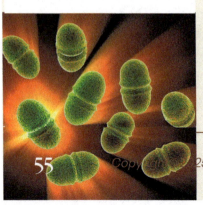

Akkermansia muciniphila
Gut benefits:

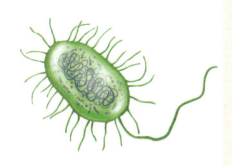

Akkermansia muciniphila is a recently discovered probiotic but it is keystone strain.
The absence of this bacterium, or being deficient in it, has been associated with obesity, metabolic issues and GI disorders to even neurodegenerative issues.
Akkermansia is the only strain that we know to date that lives in the gut lining.
It is a mucin-degrading bacterium and has beneficial effects on the host metabolic profile. The best-described effect of Akkermansia is its ability to strengthen the integrity of the intestinal barrier to prevent leaky gut syndrome.

Akkermansia also helps to preserve the epithelial barrier's integrity by stimulating anti-inflammatory pathways. From the fermentation of mucin, Akkermansia muciniphila produces short chain fatty acids (SCFAs) such a propionate and acetate, which are used to fuel other strains of healthy bacteria.
It is very important to have a strong gut lining, and therefore, it is so important to have Akkermansia. A strong gut lining protects you from developing gut dysbiosis and chronic illness over time.

CAUTIONARY NOTICE:
Conditions like inflammatory bowel disease (IBD), Salmonella typhimurium infection or post-antibiotic reconstitution may not benefit from Akkermansia supplementation.
Using Akkermansia in patients with higher risk of developing IBD, like those with endocrine and gynaecological disorders—such as polycystic ovary syndrome (PCOS) or endometriosis— should be critically evaluated.
Patients with Parkinson's disease or Multiple Sclerosis should avoid Akkermansia supplementation, because their gut microbiota exhibits a characteristic signature of Akkermansia municiphila in abundance.

4. REPAIR THE GUT LINING

Repair the intestinal lining by supplying key nutrients that are often deficient in a disease state.

The term "leaky gut" is popular nowadays but not everyone knows the definition. **"Leaky gut" means increased intestinal permeability.** This is a condition in which the gaps between the cells of your gut lining become bigger. The lining of a healthy intestine is semipermeable. This means that it only lets through water and nutrients and acts as a barrier against pathogenic bacteria and toxins.

If you have increased intestinal permeability, larger molecules, like chemicals, toxins, and microbes may pass through your gut barrier into your bloodstream causing health problems.

To prevent a "leaky gut" you need to repair the gut lining, with a healthy diet, and some supplements.

SUPPLEMENTS FOR HEALTHY GUT LINING

Multivitamin ADEK (containing vitamins A, D, E, K)

Vitamin A
Vitamin A helps protect the gut lining from damage and is important for a healthy immune system.

Vitamin A plays a protective role against infections thanks to its ability to enhance antibody responses, especially IgA antibody responses in mucosal tissues. IgA is secreted into the gut lining and provides protection against harmful pathogens helping maintain a healthy microbiome.

Vitamin D
Vitamin D plays an important role in immune function and cell division. There are vitamin D receptors in the gut lining that communicate with the tight junctions that stitch the gut cells together.

Vitamin E
Vitamin E helps protect the gut lining from damage caused by free radicals. Its anti-inflammatory properties also may reduce digestive inflammation.

Vitamin K2
Some studies show that vitamin K2 improves the beneficial gut microbiome and reduces intestinal inflammation and oxidative stress.

Collagen peptides

A recent study found that collagen peptides can prevent further breakdown of the intestinal lining. Collagen plays an essential role in strengthening the lining of our gut, helping to maintain its structure and permeability.

Probiotics

The role of probiotics is explained above.

Omega 3

A study published in the European Journal of Nutrition has found that omega-3 fatty acids may help improve the integrity of the intestinal barrier. Omega 3 fatty acids nourish a healthy microbiome and increase the diversity of healthy gut bacteria. A lack of diversity in your gut bacteria has been linked to IBS symptoms and even colon cancer.

To improve the integrity of the intestinal barrier, supplementation of high-quality fish oil or Algae Oil (vegan) is recommended.

Fiber and butyrate

The healthy bacteria in your gut feed on fiber. In particular, your gut bacteria like a specific type of plant fiber called **prebiotics.**

When fiber is fermented by the gut bacteria, it creates a short-chain amino acid called **butyrate.** Research from 2015 has discovered that butyrate supplementation may stimulate mucus production and improve tight junctions in the lining of the gut.

Common types of prebiotic compounds include:

1. **Inulin**: Found in foods like chicory root, Jerusalem artichokes, bananas, onions, and garlic.

2. **Fructo-oligosaccharides (FOS)**: Present in foods such as garlic, onions, leeks, asparagus, and bananas.

3. **Galacto-oligosaccharides (GOS)**: Found in legumes (beans, lentils) and some grains.

4. **Resistant starch:** Found in underripe bananas, cooked and cooled potatoes, legumes, and some grains.

Black Garlic

Black garlic is a type of aged garlic that is made by placing garlic in a warm, moist, controlled environment over several weeks.

Many studies demonstrated that the consumption of black garlic can modulate the gut microbiota by enhancing probiotics' growth and suppressing pathogenic microorganisms' growth. This supplement can modulate gene expression in the gut and the gut microbiome.

Garlic can be considered as a great functional food containing bioactive constituents and antiinflammatory, lipid-lowering, glucose-lowering, and antihypertensive agents. Garlic shows antibacterial and antifungal properties. It is effective against bacteria, like Enterococcus, Helicobacter pylori, Escherichia coli, Staphylococcus aureus, Salmonella typhimurium, Vibrio cholera, Methicillin-resistant Staphylococcus aureus strains and fungus-like, Epidermophyton, Trichophyton, Cryptococcus and Candida.

Black garlic can regulate blood glucose levels, preventing serious health issues, such as acne, diabetes, kidney dysfunction, and more.

Some research show that black garlic lowers markers of liver injury, decreases fatty deposits in the liver, and improves liver function.

CAUTIONARY NOTICE:
Patients with impaired sulfur metabolism should not supplement garlic because is high in sulfur. If you feel bloated after consuming garlic, do not use it.

Vitamin C

Vitamin C is an antioxidant that can reduce damage from inflammation. It is also needed for the production of collagen, an important protein that keeps your gut lining healthy.

Magnesium

Magnesium promotes a healthy balance of bacteria in your intestines and helps regulate muscle contractions in the digestive tract.

Zinc

A 2001 study found that zinc supplementation can help to strengthen the gut lining in patients with Crohn's disease. Other research from 2015 shows that zinc can modify the tight junctions of the intestinal lining, helping to reduce gut permeability.

CAUTIONARY NOTICE
Avoid zinc overdosing. It is recommended to check your zinc level before long-term use (from a blood test or Elemental Hair Analysis).

L-glutamine

Glutamine is an amino acid which is best known for helping to repair the intestinal lining.
Research from 2015 indicates that glutamine can improve the growth and survival of enterocytes - cells that line the inner surface of the small and large intestines. It may also regulate the function of the intestinal barrier during stress.

CAUTIONARY NOTICE
Avoid using if concerned by:
- Liver disease- Glutamine can increase the risk of brain dysfunction in people with advanced liver disease
- Bipolar disorder- Glutamine might increase the risk of mania or hypomania in people with Bipolar disorder
- Monosodium glutamate (MSG) sensitivity- If you are sensitive to MSG, you might also be sensitive to glutamine (the body converts glutamine to glutamate)
- Seizures- Glutamine might increase the likelihood of seizures in some people. Avoid use if you are at risk of having a seizure

Berberine

Berberine has been used in the treatment of inflammatory bowel diseases.
An animal study from 2015 indicates that berberine was able to alleviate the changes in intestinal mucus in rats.

Consult health practitioner to choose the best supplements for your needs.

5. REBALANCE YOUR GUT HEALTH

Rebalancing your gut health is crucial for maintenance and prevention of future health issues. This includes retaining healthy gut function by continuing a healthy diet and exercising, managing stress, having good quality sleep, and continuing some of the supplements. I will address a healthy diet in the next chapter.

STRESS AND MICROBIOME

The relationship between stress and the microbiome is bidirectional. The microbiome impacts the way your body responds to stress but stress impacts the microbiome.
Stress also alters motility (the movement in the gut). Motility is one of the factors which keeps the microbiome well organised. Stress also may deplete certain bacteria.

The microbiome impacts the way your body responds to stress but stress impacts the microbiome too.

The microbes in the gut have receptors for the stress hormones adrenaline and norepinephrine. When we are under stress, the signals also go directly to the microbes. This changes the expression of their genes and the behaviour of the microbes in the gut. When the microbial balance is disturbed, leaky gut syndrome can develop.

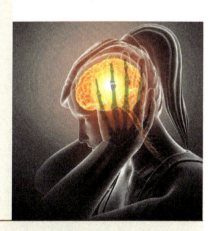

SLEEP AND IMMUNE SYSTEM

Lack of sleep can affect your immune system. Studies show that people who don't get quality sleep or enough sleep are more likely to get ill after being exposed to a virus or to develop chronic health problems, including skin disorders.

Blue light, the kind emitted by our phones, computer screens and tablets, seems to be particularly disruptive to melatonin production. Melatonin is a hormone made in the body that regulates night and day cycles or sleep-wake cycles. New research shows that blue light exposure significantly reduces the amount of melatonin secreted by the brain's pineal gland. This has noxious effects on both the duration, as well as the quality of sleep.

TIPS ON HOW TO IMPROVE YOUR SLEEP

- consistent wake-up time
- direct sunlight exposure in the morning
- stop caffeine at 2 pm
- no alcohol 3h before bedtime
- lowering the temperature in the bedroom for the night
- limiting exposure to blue light 2 hours before bedtime
- using a blue light filter on your electronic device.

CHAPTER NINE SUMMARY

9.2. TIPS TO IMPROVE GUT HEALTH

People with skin problems have gut dysbiosis, an imbalance in the intestinal microbiome. This discovery indicates a link between gut health and acne, thus healing your gut will improve your skin condition.

GUT HEALING PROGRAMME

1. IDENTIFY AND REMOVE THE POTENTIAL UNDERLYING CAUSES OF THE GUT IMBALANCE

This relates to inflammatory foods and/or disbiotic/pathogenic microbes in the gut. A test used to diagnose food sensitivities and commonly available is the food IgG test. Unfortunately, the IgG test does not detect all types of food sensitivities. There is another cellular test that check immune cells respond to food products. This test measures the total amount of inflammation caused by food substance, while IgG antibody testing measures antibodies, but not inflammation.

In some cases, gluten can be involved in acne development. Studies show links between coeliac disease and several other skin conditions, including acne, eczema, psoriasis and urticaria.

Regarding problematic microbes or pathogens, testing is the best way to identify if gut infection is caused by dysbiotic bacteria, yeasts, or parasites. The Comprehensive Stool Analysis with Parasitology and PCR evaluates the status of beneficial bacteria, imbalanced commensal bacteria, pathogenic bacteria, parasites and yeasts like Candida.

Removing them using natural anti-microbial supplements or with medication is an important step in reducing inflammation.

2. INTRODUCE NUTRIENTS AND SUPPLEMENTS THAT SUPPORT THE BREAKDOWN AND ABSORPTION OF FOOD

Use certain supplements that support the breakdown and absorption of food, like HCl (stomach acid), digestive enzymes, bile support, short-chain fatty acids (like butyrate) or anti-inflammatory supplements. Discuss with a Functional Medicine Practitioner or other IBS practitioner what will work best for you.

It is also important to support liver function. The liver can affect acne through its role in fat digestion. Poor liver function can lead to increased fats in your bloodstream, which can increase sebum production and clog your pores, causing breakouts and acne. The liver health affects hormonal balance too. Poor liver function can lead to hormonal acne because it does not regulate hormone levels in the bloodstream effectively. Toxins in the liver can overload this organ, leading to poor liver detoxification. This is another way poor liver function affects skin conditions like acne vulgaris, rosacea and psoriasis. To support your liver change your diet and supplement Milk Thistle or Artichoke Leaf Extract.

3. REPOPULATE YOUR BENEFICIAL BACTERIA

Repopulate your beneficial bacteria using prebiotic and probiotic-rich foods and good quality muti-strained probiotic supplements.

Below are examples of probiotic strains beneficial for the gut.

Lactobacillus
Bifidobacterium
Bacillus
Saccharomyces Boulardii
Enterococcus faecalis
Akkermansia muciniphila

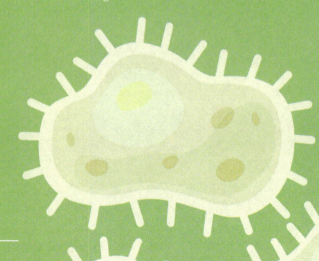

Copyright©2025 Katarzyna Blochowiak This book is registered with Protect My Work

4. REPAIR THE GUT LINING

Repair the gut lining with targeted supplements, which supply key nutrients that can often be deficient in a disease state.

Supplements for healthy gut lining

ADEK (Vitamins A, D, E, K2)
Collagen peptides
Probiotics
Omega 3
Fiber and butyrate
Black Garlic
Vitamin C
Magnesium
Zinc
L-glutamine
Berberine

5. REBALANCE YOUR GUT HEALTH

Rebalancing your gut health includes retaining healthy gut function by continuing a healthy diet and exercising, managing stress, having good quality sleep and continuing some of the supplements.

CHAPTER TEN

HOW TO RESTORE ORAL MICROBIOME

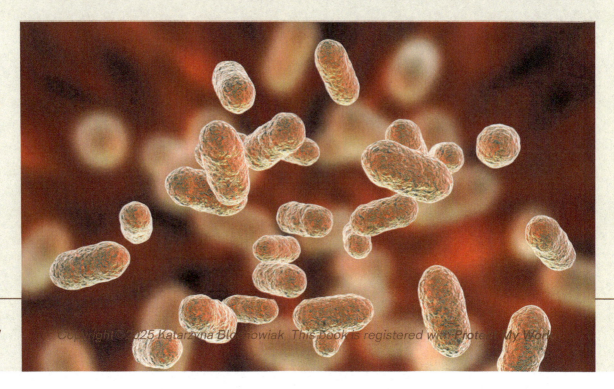

Studies show that brushing the teeth after meals significantly reduces the levels of Candida albicans (yeast) in the stool. Candida albicans colonizes the gastrointestinal tract from the mouth. **Patients with gastrointestinal disorders should take care of their oral hygiene.** Another interesting fact is that the fungal component of dental plaque has been shown to be dominated by Candida albicans. Good oral hygiene, elimination of plaque and reduction of consumption of refined sugars may reduce significantly the levels of Candida albicans in stool.

Studies demonstrate that people with a higher plaque index, which indicates poor oral hygiene, are at higher risk of developing autoimmune disorders, like acne.
The teeth surface is an ideal place for biofilms (plaque) development. **Dental plaque is the most common example of biofilm.** Biofilm is a community of microbial cells surrounded by a secreted polymer, called the extracellular polymerisubstance (EPS) which is endotoxin (a toxin of internal origin, e.g. produced by bacteria). Biofilms are created by multiple organisms, including bacteria, viruses and fungal species. Biofilm bacteria are able to resist up to 5000 times the antibiotic concentration that normally is needed. Periodontal disease is the most common oral disease associated with a highly pathogenic biofilm that triggers an inflammatory response of the immune system. The plaque biofilm is not naturally shed, which leads to dysbiosis in the absence of proper oral hygiene to remove it. If not removed, certain bacteria multiply and dysbiosis develops. That is why both regular teeth brushing and removing plaque in the dental clinic is important for oral health and acne prevention.

You can also choose **dental plaque remover toothpaste.**
The mechanical action of brushing combined with the antimicrobial ingredients of the toothpaste helps to improve the oral microbiome.

Other toothpastes worth to consider are toothpastes with probiotics.

Toothpaste with probiotics nourishes your oral microbiome. Often they contain other natural plant-based ingredients that support your microbiome too.

Oral probiotics could be very effective in improving your oral microbiome.

I recommend chewable **dental probiotics with Streptococcus Salivarius K12 (BLIS K12).**
Streptococcus salivarius is a gram-positive bacterium that is part of the normal human oral microflora, predominantly colonising the tongue.

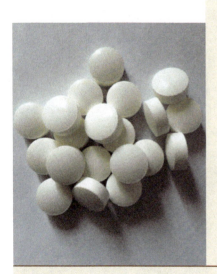

This strain has been shown to inhibit the growth of Cutibacterium acnes and to decrease inflammatory markers that are associated with acne.
Streptococcus salivarius K12 demonstrates also other health benefits. This probiotic is intended for use in oral cavities, combating bad breath and gum disease. Streptococcus salivarius K12 has the potential to improve oral diseases and mucosal barrier function and prevent upper respiratory tract infections (URTI).

Dental probiotics also contain other scientifically researched probiotic strains, like Lactobacillus Salivarius, Lactobacillus Acidophillus, Lactobacillus Brevis, Lactobacillus Paracasei, Lactobacillus Reuteri, and Streptococcus Thermophilus. **These supplements are** effective in eliminating bad breath, oral thrush, and support healthy gum. Overgrowth of pathogenic oral bacteria is the most common cause of gum disease. Combat the dysbiosis in the mouth by colonising it with good bacteria.

You can improve your oral health too with Coconut Oil Pulling.
Coconut oil pulling reduces the amount of harmful bacteria in your mouth and decreases your risk of some health conditions, like acne. Oil pulling has been used for thousands of years as an Indian folk remedy. To start oil pulling you have to put one tablespoon of coconut oil in your mouth and swish the oil around your mouth for about 15 minutes. Then spit out the oil (do not swallow it) and brush your teeth.
Streptococcus mutans is one of the harmful bacteria in your mouth involved in plaque buildup and tooth decay. One study from 2016 showed that coconut oil pulling for 10 minutes daily significantly reduced the number of Streptococcus mutans in saliva in 2 weeks, compared to distilled water. Another study from 2020 showed that coconut oil pulling was effective at decreasing the accumulation of plaque.

CHAPTER TEN
SUMMARY

HOW TO RESTORE ORAL MICROBIOME

The teeth surface is an ideal place for biofilms (plaque) development. Dental plaque is the most common example of biofilm. Biofilm is a community of microbial cells surrounded by a secreted polymer, called the extracellular polymerisubstance (EPS).

The plaque biofilm is not naturally shed, which leads to dysbiosis in the absence of proper oral hygiene to remove it. If not removed, certain bacteria multiply and dysbiosis develops. That is why both regular teeth brushing and removing plaque in the dental clinic are important for oral health and acne prevention.

You can choose dental plaque remover toothpaste. Other toothpastes worth **considering** are toothpastes with probiotics.

Oral probiotics could be effective in improving your oral microbiome too. I recommend chewable d**ental probiotics with Streptococcus salivarius BLIS K12.** Streptococcus salivarius K12 has been shown to inhibit the growth of Cutibacterium acnes and to decrease inflammatory markers that are associated with acne.

You can improve your oral health too with **Coconut Oil Pulling.** Coconut oil pulling reduces the amount of harmful bacteria in your mouth and decreases your risk of acne. To start oil pulling you have to put one tablespoon of coconut oil in your mouth and swish the oil around your mouth for about 15 minutes. Then spit out the oil (do not swallow it) and brush your teeth.

CHAPTER ELEVEN

ACNE AND DIET

What you eat significantly affects your skin health.

Acne vulgaris is closely related to the Western diet.

11.1. FIVE MAJOR FOOD CLASSES AND FACTORS THAT PROMOTE ACNE

1) hyperglycemic carbohydrates,
2) milk and dairy products,
3) trans fatty acids (TFAs)
4) diet deficient in omega-3 polyunsaturated fatty acids
5) diet that disturbs the bacterial balance in the gut - a diet low in fiber, exposure to pesticides, herbicides, and preservatives, consumption of antibiotics and other medications, alcohol, or drugs.

Populations exposed to a paleolithic diet (low glycemic load, no milk and dairy consumption, natural food) such as the Ache hunters in Paraguay, the Inuit, the Kitavan islanders of Papua New Guinea, and adolescents of rural areas of Brazil are examples of acne-free populations. An increase in acne prevalence has been reported for Okinawa islanders, Inuits, and Chinese after a transition from their traditional diets to Western diets. More and more clinical, epidemiological, and translational evidence emphasizes the impact of nutritional factors in the pathogenesis of acne vulgaris.

Acne vulgaris is closely related to the Western diet.

According to Burris acne severity in a cohort of New York young people was associated with 1) increased intake of carbohydrates (high glycemic load), 2) number of milk and dairy servings per day, and 3) amount of saturated fat and trans-fatty acid (TFA) intake.

Below I am explaining why the above factors contribute to acne development so heavily.

1) Hyperglycemic carbohydrates

Many studies found a positive correlation between a high glycemic index and acne.

The glycaemic index (GI) is a system of ranking carbohydrate-containing foods based on how slowly or quickly they can increase blood glucose levels. Examples of food high in GI to avoid, include white and whole wheat bread, white rice, breakfast cereals and cereal bars, cookies, cakes, potatoes and chips, rice crackers and sweetened dairy products such as sweetened yogurts.

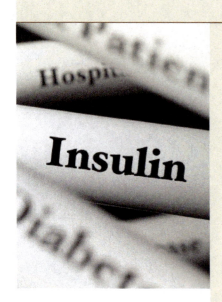

Foods with **high glycemic index** contain a lot of sugar or heavily processed grains, like white bread, and cause the production of insulin in the body. **Insulin, in turn, breaks down collagen and also promotes androgen synthesis, resulting in excessive sebum production, causing acne severity.** A study from 2015 demonstrated that a low-glycemic index diet improves skin condition as well as insulin sensitivity in young males with acne vulgaris. It means that insulin and carbohydrate metabolism may affect the severity of acne.

Other studies show that the majority of acne patients have insulin resistance. They have significantly higher levels of insulin biomarkers, C-peptide, and TyG index, compared to control candidates. C-peptide is a byproduct the pancreas releases into the body when it makes insulin. High C-peptide levels mean the body is making a lot of insulin. The triglyceride glucose (TyG) index is a marker of insulin resistance. There is a positive and strong correlation between the level of C-peptide and TyG index biomarkers and the severity of acne.

Studies show that the majority of acne patients have insulin resistance.

We recommend controlling the dietary risk factors that increase insulin resistance during the acne treatment period, as well as encouraging physicians to look for these biomarkers when assessing acne severity.

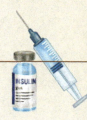

75 Copyright©2025 Katarzyna Blochowiak This book is registered with **Protect My Work**

Scientists observed a linear correlation between serum **IGF-1 (Insulin-like Growth Factor-1)** concentrations and facial sebum excretion rates of male acne patients. Remarkably, increased serum IGF-1 levels have been also detected in women with post-adolescent acne.

Many foods with a high glycemic load increase IGF-1 and insulin levels, which affects the expression of FoxO1. The FoxO1 is a protein that plays a major role in regulating the insulin response. FoxO1 is inhibited by insulin, so high insulin means low FoxO1. A FoxO1 deficiency is a key factor in acne development and promotes lipogenesis (excess sebum production), secretion of proinflammatory cytokines and rapid production of new keratinocytes - cells that form the epithelium. A diet high in carbohydrates stimulates lipogenesis in adipocytes (fat cells) while fasting reduces it. Glucose stimulates lipogenesis by insulin secretion and by dysregulation of several lipogenic genes.

Many foods with a high glycemic load increase IGF-1 (Insulin-like Growth Factor-1) and insulin levels.

It means that a high carbohydrate diet promotes acne. Scientists agree that a high intake of refined carbohydrates is a main factor in acne pathogenesis. The effect of high glycemic diets on the induction and the severity of acne has been proved by several studies. Hyperglycemic carbohydrates modulate the bioactivity of free serum IGF-1 and free serum androgens.

What is important to note, is that a decrease in sebaceous gland size and reduced severity in facial acne skin was observed after an intervention of 10 weeks long low glycemic load diet.

High carbohydrate diet promotes acne.

A recent study shows an association between IGF-I (CA) gene polymorphism and acne development. But genetic mutation does not mean that you have to suffer from acne. Scientific evidence points to the predominance of environmental and epigenetic factors.

A recent study shows an association between IGF-I (CA) gene polymorphism and acne development.

A study from 2013 found that the frequency of genotype IGF-1 (CA) was significantly higher in acne patients than in the control group. A strong association between IGF-I (CA) genotypes and severity of acne was found.

But genetic mutation does not mean that you have to suffer from acne. **Scientific evidence points to the predominance of environmental and epigenetic factors. Epigenetics is the study of how your behaviors, diet, lifestyle, and environment can affect the way your genes work.**

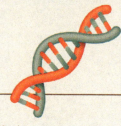

2) Milk and dairy products.

Dairy-protein-based diets provide more leucine than diets rich in plants. Leucine is an amino acid that stimulates some pathways, which causes **excess sebum production and activates acne development.**

Dairy-protein-based diets also **increase the inflammation associated with acne**. Another thing worth mentioning is that plant-based diets promote the diversity of the intestinal microbiome, improving overall health. This also can prevent the development of acne because the gut microbiome modulates the inflammatory response.

Milk proteins have **insulinotropic properties,** which means they can stimulate or affect the production and activity of insulin. The whey fraction contains the predominating insulin secretagogue.

There is evidence that hyperglycemic carbohydrates and insulinotropic milk and dairy products may promote acne development by encouraging **insulin growth factor-1 (IGF-1)** signaling, which proves the link between milk products and acne.

In 1885, Bulkley published his study reporting the acne-aggravating effects of milk, involving 1,500 patients with this skin disorder. Harvard epidemiologist Adebamowo also provided evidence for the association between milk consumption and acne.

Dairy products may promote acne development by encouraging insulin growth factor-1 (IGF-1) signaling.

Another study involving 563 patients showed, that moderate-to-severe adolescent acne was closely associated with high consumption of milk, particularly skimmed milk, cheese, yogurts, sweets, and cakes, low consumption of fish, and limited intake of fruits and vegetables. Such a diet is the opposite of Paleolithic nutrition.

Increased IGF-1 production caused by milk protein intake is thus superimposed on exaggerated IGF-1 signaling of puberty. This explains **the earlier onset of puberty and the persistence of acne in the third decade of life in milk-consuming populations.**

3) Trans fatty acids (TFAs)

Industrially produced **trans-fatty acids (TFAs) are manufactured fats created during a process called hydrogenation. TFAs have been found to aggravate acne.**

These partially hydrogenated fats have displaced natural solid fats and liquid oils in many foods and can be found in fast food, fried food, snack food and baked goods - those have all been associated with acne.

Trans fats products include:

- fast food, e.g. fries
- powdered soups and sauces
- margarine
- bread
- chips, sticks, crackers
- cakes, cookies

Trans-fatty acids are manufactured fats created during a process called hydrogenation. TFAs have been found to aggravate acne.

4) Diet deficient in omega-3 polyunsaturated fatty acids

Fish consumption shows the acne-preventive effect. This effect is well documented and explained by the anti-inflammatory effects of omega-3 fatty acids present in fish. One case study showed an overall improvement in acne severity with a 12-week daily supplementation of 3 g fish oil.

Burris and Jung observed an aggravation of acne with an increased intake of saturated fat, whereas a higher intake of fish, which is rich in omega-3 fatty acids, showed an acne-protective effect.

Omega-3 fatty acids exert anti-inflammatory effects, including the downregulation of pro-inflammatory cytokines, and insulin-like growth factor-1. Therefore, they may improve acne severity.

Cold-water fatty fish, such as salmon, mackerel, tuna, herring and sardines, contain the highest amounts of omega-3s.

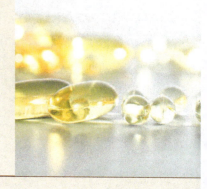

Diet is a decisive factor in the development of acne because it is related to the composition and diversity of the intestinal microbiome.

5) Diet that disturbs the bacterial balance in the gut.

Diet is a decisive factor in the development of acne because it is related to the composition and diversity of the intestinal microbiome.

A Western diet rich in ultra-processed foods, chemicals, trans fats, and refined sugars has a negative impact on the gut microbiome and is a risk factor for acne aggravation. Many studies show that foods with a high glycemic index/load, and trans fat promote the formation of acne lesions and change the composition of intestinal bacteria, while the intake of vegetables and fruits improves gut health. Bad eating habits, and exposure to pesticides, herbicides, preservatives, antibiotics or other medications, as well as alcohol or drugs lead to a disturbed bacterial balance. Artificial sweeteners can also cause gut and skin inflammation, acne breakouts, pimples or blocked pores.

Changes in the composition of the microflora induce increased permeability of the intestinal barrier and stimulate the immune system, leading to systemic inflammation, which impairs skin condition.

CHAPTER ELEVEN SUMMARY

11.1. ACNE AND DIET

What you eat significantly affects your skin health.
Acne vulgaris is closely related to the Western diet.

Populations exposed to a paleolithic diet (low glycemic load, no milk and dairy consumption, natural food) such as the Ache hunters in Paraguay, the Inuit, the Kitavan islanders of Papua New Guinea, and adolescents of rural areas of Brazil are examples of acne-free populations.

FIVE MAJOR FOOD CLASSES AND FACTORS THAT PROMOTE ACNE ARE:

1) hyperglycemic carbohydrates

Foods with high glycemic index contain a lot of sugar or heavily processed grains, like white bread, and cause insulin production in the body. Insulin, in turn, breaks down collagen and also promotes androgen synthesis, resulting in excessive sebum production and causing acne severity.

Studies show that the majority of acne patients have insulin resistance. Many foods with a high glycemic load increase IGF-1 (Insulin-like Growth Factor-1) and insulin levels, causing insulin resistance. Scientific evidence shows that IGF-1 plays the primary role in acne development.

Food high in GI to avoid, include white and whole wheat bread, white rice, breakfast cereals and cereal bars, cookies, cakes, potatoes and chips, rice crackers and sweetened dairy products such as sweetened yogurts.

2) milk and dairy products

Dairy-protein-based diets provide more leucine than diets rich in plants. Leucine is an amino acid that stimulates excess sebum production which activates acne development.

Milk proteins have insulinotropic properties, which means they can stimulate or affect the production and activity of insulin.

There is evidence that hyperglycemic carbohydrates and milk and dairy products may promote acne development by increasing insulin-like growth factor-1 (IGF-1).

Increased IGF-1 production caused by milk protein intake is thus superimposed on exaggerated IGF-1 levels of puberty.

3) trans fatty acids (TFAs)

Trans-fatty acids are manufactured fats created during a process called hydrogenation. TFAs have been found to aggravate acne.

Trans fats products include:
fast food, e.g. fries, powdered soups and sauces, margarine, bread, chips, sticks, crackers, cakes and cookies.

4) diet deficient in omega-3 polyunsaturated fatty acids

Fish consumption is shown to prevent acne through the anti-inflammatory effects of omega-3 fatty acids present in fish.

Omega-3 fatty acids exert anti-inflammatory effects, including the downregulation of pro-inflammatory cytokines and insulin-like growth factor-1 (IGF-1).

5) diet that disturbs the bacterial balance in the gut

Diet is a decisive factor in the development of acne because it is related to the composition and diversity of the intestinal microbiome.

A Western diet rich in ultra-processed foods, chemicals, trans fats, and refined sugars has a negative impact on the gut microbiome and is a risk factor for acne aggravation. Bad eating habits, and exposure to pesticides, herbicides, preservatives, antibiotics or other medications, as well as alcohol or drugs, lead to a disturbed bacterial balance.

Changes in the composition of the microflora induce increased permeability of the intestinal barrier and stimulate the immune system, leading to systemic inflammation, which impairs skin condition.

II.2. NUTRITIONAL THERAPY OF ACNE

In 2005, Cordain emphasized **the beneficial effects of a paleolithic diet for treating acne.** A paleolithic diet is a nutritional plan based on foods humans might have eaten during the Paleolithic Era. The Paleolithic Era dates from around 2.5 million to 10,000 years ago.

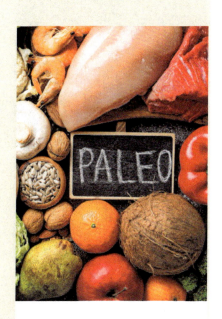

A modern paleo diet includes vegetables, fruits, fish, eggs, lean meats, nuts and seeds. People could get these foods in the Paleolithic Era by hunting and gathering. This diet does not include foods that became more common when small-scale farming began about 10,000 years ago, like grains, legumes and dairy products.

As mentioned previously, the acne-preventive effect of fish consumption is well explained by the anti-inflammatory effects of omega-3 fatty acids.

Plant-derived natural compounds, such as the green tea polyphenol EGCG and the resveratrol (polyphenol from red grapes and berries), are also helpful in fighting acne. EGCG suppresses IGF-1-induced lipogenesis (excess sebum production), explaining the improvement of acne.

In 2005, Cordain emphasized the beneficial effects of a paleolithic diet for treating acne.

Resveratrol is a polyphenolic flavonoid from grapes, berries and red wine that inhibits the growth of Cutibacterium acnes. Importantly, resveratrol also inhibited sebocyte growth. Sebocytes are sebum-producing epithelial cells.

Food influences the activity of the human genome. Genome is the complete set of genetic material in an organism.

Acne is caused by imbalanced nutrigenomics induced by a Western diet, which exaggerates insulin/IGF-1 response. **Nutrigenomics defines the relationship between nutrients, diet, and gene expression.**

The epidemic of acne vulgaris is a systemic disease of Western civilisation, similar to diabetes or obesity. Acne patients should control their intake of sugar and refined carbohydrates, milk, whey and casein protein supplements, not forgetting about avoiding trans-fats.

The ideal "anti-acne diet" is a paleolithic-like nutrition with an accentuated intake of vegetables and fruits with low glycemic index and sea fish as an Omega 3-fatty acids source. An acne-preventive diet should contain plant-derived natural acne inhibitors such as green tea (EGCG), resveratrol (berries and grapes), curcumin (turmeric) and silymarin (milk thistle).

Food influences the activity of the human genome. Genome is the complete set of genetic material in an organism.

CAUTIONARY NOTICE
Green tea is not recommended for children under 14 years of age.
No studies are showing whether or not it is safe to give milk thistle to a child.

Eating a balanced nutritional diet, rich in vitamins, minerals, and antioxidants, is a key factor in promoting skin health. Vitamins A, C, D, E, B2, B3, B6, zinc, and selenium are necessary for optimal skin health.

A healthy skin diet is a diet that provides all the necessary nutrients needed for cell growth.

Many fruits and vegetables contain compounds that can benefit your skin. More and more scientists confirm that what you eat can significantly affect the health and ageing of your skin.

Eating a balanced nutritional diet, rich in vitamins, minerals, and anti-oxidants, is a key factor in promoting skin health.

Eat five portions of fruit and vegetables a day.

BELOW ARE SOME TIPS REGARDING A HEALTHY SKIN DIET PREVENTING ACNE

- **Eat five portions of fruit and vegetables a day** – choose colorful fruit and vegetables to provide your skin with a diverse range of vitamins, minerals, and antioxidants, like broccoli, spinach, cauliflower, bok choy and cabbage. Red grapes and berries contain resveratrol, which shows antioxidant properties and can neutralise free radicals preventing skin damage and signs of ageing.

- **Consume food rich in omega-3**

  What foods provide omega-3s?

  - Fish and other seafood (especially cold-water fatty fish, such as salmon, herring, mackerel, tuna and sardines)
  - Flaxseed oil
  - Nuts and seeds (such as chia seeds, flaxseed and walnuts)

- **Drink plenty of water** – your skin needs water to stay hydrated. You need six to eight glasses of water a day.

- **Drink green tea** – contains plant-derived natural acne inhibitors such as EGCG. Green tea is not recommended for children under 14 years of age.

- **Consume products high in vitamin C** – vitamin C is necessary for skin healing and a strong immune system. In addition to its antioxidant functions, vitamin C regulates the synthesis of collagen. Collagen is a major component of your skin.
Consume plenty of foods rich in vitamin C, like blueberries, blackcurrants, kiwi, strawberries, oranges, papaya, broccoli, peppers, brussels sprouts and sweet potatoes.

- **Consume enough vitamin E** – vitamin E protects your skin from cell damage and it supports healthy skin growth. Consume plenty of foods rich in vitamin E, including red sweet peppers, turnip, greens, beet greens, spinach, butternut squash, avocado, mango, hazelnuts, pine nuts and sunflower seeds.

- **Consume enough beta carotene** - red and yellow peppers, carrots, and butternut squash contain a lot of beta carotene which the body converts to vitamin A. Vitamin A prevents skin cell damage.

- **Consume food rich in zinc** - zinc has anti-inflammatory properties and can reduce the swelling and redness caused by acne. It also helps to reduce sebum production. Zinc-rich foods include flaxseeds, pumpkin seeds, egg yolks and dark chocolate.

Copyright©2025 Katarzyna Blochowiak This book is registered with **Protect My Work**

- **Consume food rich in selenium** - selenium protects the skin against acne, UV damage, pigmentation and inflammation. Food sources of selenium are walnuts Brazil nuts, fish, shellfish, white meat, potatoes, lentils, peas, tomatoes and broccoli.

- **Consume prebiotic and probiotic food** - Prebiotics are substances supporting the multiplication and growth of beneficial intestinal bacteria, like chicory inulin, onion, garlic, leek Jerusalem artichoke and algae (spirulina and chlorella).

Probiotics are live bacteria and yeasts which provide many health benefits and improve gut and overall health.

Examples of products containing probiotics

- dairy-free yogurt
- kimchi
- kombucha
- natto
- sauerkraut
- brined olives

CAUTIONARY NOTICE
People with yeast overgrowth and with high histamine (those with allergic reactions) do not tolerate fermented food and should avoid it.

Consume prebiotic and probiotic food.

CHAPTER ELEVEN SUMMARY

11.2. NUTRITIONAL THERAPY OF ACNE

The diet most beneficial for acne is a paleolithic diet. A paleolithic diet is a nutritional plan based on foods humans might have eaten during the Paleolithic Era. A modern paleo diet includes vegetables, fruits, fish, eggs, lean meats, nuts and seeds.

The acne-preventive effect of fish consumption is well explained by the anti-inflammatory effects of omega-3 fatty acids. Plant-derived natural compounds, such as the green tea polyphenol EGCG and the resveratrol (a polyphenol from red grapes and berries), turmeric and milk thistle are also helpful in fighting acne.

Food influences the activity of the human genome. Genome is the complete set of genetic material in an organism.

Acne is the result of imbalanced nutrigenomics induced by a Western diet, that exaggerates insulin/IGF-1 response. Nutrigenomics defines the relationship between nutrients, diet and gene expression.

Eating a balanced nutritional diet, rich in vitamins, minerals and antioxidants, is a key factor in promoting skin health.

Below are some tips regarding a healthy skin diet preventing acne.

- Eat five portions of fruit and vegetables a day
- Consume food rich in omega-3, like fish
- Drink plenty of water
- Drink green tea
- Consume products high in vitamin C
- Consume enough vitamin E
- Consume enough beta carotene
- Consume food rich in zinc
- Consume food rich in selenium
- Consume prebiotic and probiotic food

CHAPTER TWELVE

HORMONES AND ACNE

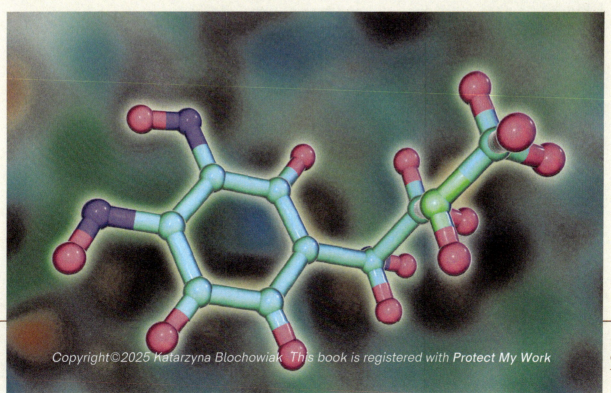

Acne usually begins in **adolescence**, when a considerable hormonal change occurs in young people. **There is an increase in androgen production in the body and a local increase in androgen production at the skin level.**

The androgen receptor is present in many skin cells, such as sebocytes and follicular keratinocytes. Increased androgen production at the skin can generate an increase in sebum production. There is a greater expression of the androgen receptor in the areas of the skin where acne lesions appear.

Acne correlates with increased sebum production. Insulin, GH (Growth hormone), and IGF-1 (Insulin-like Growth Factor-1) increase sebaceous gland growth, differentiation and sebaceous lipogenesis. Lipogenesis is the formation of fats from surplus glucose.

The main hormone that controls pubertal development is Insulin-like growth factor 1 (IGF-1). IGF-1 is a hormone that manages the effects of growth hormone (GH) in your body and increases in circulation during puberty. Both IGF-1 and GH promote normal growth of bones and tissues. Diet-induced insulin/insulin-like growth factor 1 signalling is superimposed on elevated IGF-1 levels during puberty.

Both insulin and IGF-1 activate the androgenic receptors, resulting in acne development.

Both insulin and IGF-1 activate the androgenic receptors, resulting in acne development.

After the climax of puberty, serum levels of insulin-like growth factor 1 (IGF-1) decrease continuously. Deplewski and Rosenfield in their article pointed out that serum IGF-1 levels correlate with the clinical manifestation of acne. Presented evidence shows that IGF-1 plays the primary role in acne pathogenesis. Pathogenesis is the process by which a disease or disorder develops.

IGF-1 is a potent inducer of DHEA production. DHEA is a hormone that the body uses to make androgens and estrogens. **High IGF-1 means high androgens or estrogen levels.**

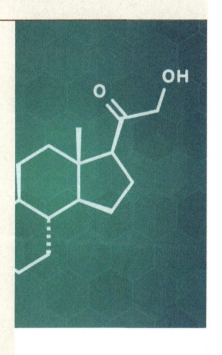

Nowadays not only young people suffer from acne. More and more adults are affected by this skin condition. Adult acne after adolescence can be persistent, recurring, or even late-onset. It affects women more often than men.

One study with more than 700 people over 25 years old, observed facial acne in 12% of women and 3% of men. It was discovered that, in these women, there was an androgenic influence caused by an increased androgen production in the ovary or adrenal glands, and also an increase in androgen production in the skin, or an increase in the sensitivity of the androgen receptor. It is more likely that the presence of acne was more correlated with the local concentration of androgens in the skin or a greater sensitivity of sebocytes to them than with blood serum concentration. Therefore the manifestation of acne in adult women would not always correlate with blood serum levels of androgens.

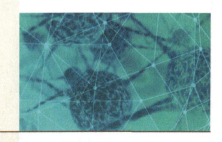

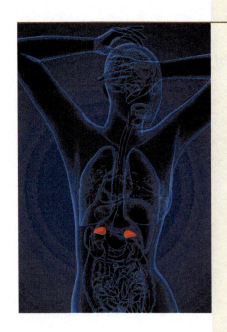

Sardana observed in 120 women over 25 years old with late-onset or persistent acne that 72% of patients had clinical hyperandrogenism, but only 18% had biochemical hyperandrogenism. Biochemical hyperandrogenism is defined as an elevated serum level of one or more androgens. It explains why in many adult women with symptoms of acne and hyperandrogenism, an increase in the concentrations of the main serum androgens (blood test) was not observed.

Acne in adult men is much less common than in women. Increased androgen-receptor sensitivity or excessive production of DHT is likely to occur in men with acne. DHT is a hormone and androgen that plays a key role in the sexual development of men.
It is confirmed that increased levels of androgens intervene essentially in acne development, but acne does not develop when there is only a loss of functionality of the androgen receptor.

Studies show that IGF-1 is the main hormone that controls pubertal development and decreases after this time. It means that we should focus on IGF-1 as a key molecule in the development of acne.

An interesting fact is that patients with Laron syndrome who have GHR (growth hormone receptor) mutations have an IGF-1 deficiency and they never develop acne. However, when they are treated with IGF-1, they develop acne. It means that for the development of acne, androgen-mediated sebum production is necessary but not sufficient.

Studies show that IGF-1 is the main hormone that controls pubertal development and decreases after this time. It means that we should focus on IGF-1 as a key molecule in the development of acne.

CHAPTER TWELVE
SUMMARY

HORMONES AND ACNE

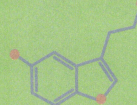

Acne usually begins in adolescence, when a considerable hormonal change occurs in young people. **There is an increase in androgen production in the body and a local increase in androgen production at the skin level.**

The androgen receptor is present in many skin cells. Increased androgen production at the skin can generate an increase in sebum production. There is a greater expression of the androgen receptor in the areas of the skin where acne lesions appear.

Insulin-like growth factor 1 (IGF-1) is a potent inducer of DHEA production. DHEA is a hormone that the body uses to make androgens and estrogens. High IGF-1 means high androgens or estrogen levels.

It is confirmed that increased levels of androgens intervene essentially in acne development, but acne does not develop when there is only a loss of functionality of the androgen receptor. Studies show that IGF-1 is the main hormone that controls pubertal development and decreases after this time. **It means that we should focus on IGF-1 as a key molecule in the development of acne.**

CHAPTER THIRTEEN

HEAVY METALS AND ACNE

Another factor involved in dermatitis and acne development is heavy metals overload, especially lead, cadmium, mercury, nickel, and arsenic are toxic to the skin. An excess copper causes acne too.

A study from 2016 shows that an increase in blood cadmium and lead may play critical roles in the pathogenesis and severity of acne vulgaris.

Heavy metals can convert the skin's sebum into a pore-blocking substance, causing acne, blackheads, redness and inflammation.

High concentrations of heavy metals in tap water, such as lead, calcium and iron can alter the skin surface chemistry and oil composition. Metals can also interact with different cleansers and soaps on our skin. Drinking unfiltered tap water can harm our overall health, affecting the skin from the inside.

Maintaining healthy detox and healthy liver function is essential to prevent acne. Another way to improve your skin's health is limiting exposure to unhealthy chemicals and heavy metals by choosing organic food, natural cosmetics, eco-cleaning products and drinking filtered water.

Minerals preventing acne include zinc, silicon and potassium.

Heavy metals testing includes Elemental Hair Analysis, Heavy Metal Blood Test or urine test.

To order Elemental Hair Analysis contact us at contact@diet-designer.com

Another factor involved in dermatitis and acne development is heavy metals overload, especially lead, cadmium, mercury, nickel, and arsenic are toxic to the skin. An excess copper causes acne too.

CHAPTER THIRTEEN
SUMMARY

HEAVY METALS AND ACNE

Another factor involved in acne development is heavy metals overload, especially lead, cadmium, mercury, nickel and arsenic are toxic to the skin. An excess copper causes acne too.

Heavy metals can convert the skin's sebum into a pore-blocking substance, causing acne, blackheads, redness and inflammation.

High concentrations of heavy metals in tap water, such as lead, calcium, and iron can alter the skin surface chemistry and oil composition. Metals can also interact with different cleansers and soaps on our skin. Drinking unfiltered tap water can harm our overall health, affecting the skin from the inside.

To improve your skin's health you need to limit exposure to unhealthy chemicals and heavy metals by choosing organic food, natural cosmetics, eco-cleaning products and drinking filtered water.

Heavy metals testing includes Elemental Hair Analysis, Heavy Metal Blood Test or urine test.

CHAPTER FOURTEEN

SUPPLEMENTS FOR HEALTHY SKIN

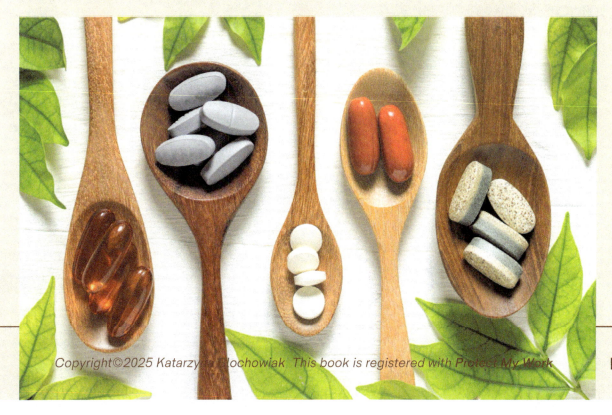

There are many natural substances, including vitamins, minerals, and plant extracts that are very effective in fighting acne and improving your skin health.

The response to herbal treatments may vary, and what works for one person may not be effective for another. It is the best idea to consult with a healthcare practitioner before choosing natural remedies, to ensure what is the best for your skin condition and overall health. Not everyone is deficient in zinc or vitamin D.

Herbal medicine for acne has been intensively researched in the past years and studies have shown promising results. Trials have found that many herbs and plants can safely reduce acne lesions and severity.

Herbal medicine for acne has been researched last years intensively, and studies have shown promising results. Trials have found that many herbs and plants can safely reduce acne lesions and severity.

FIRST CHOICE SUPPLEMENTS FOR HEALTHY SKIN

- multi-strain probiotics

Good quality multi-strain probiotics play a key role in restoring the microbiome and treating many inflammatory skin diseases. Probiotics help maintain digestive health and boost the immune system.

We recommend using probiotics with several strains to improve your gut microbiome. Some manufacturers offer good quality probiotic supplements containing more than 15 and even 30 strains.

A strain especially beneficial for the skin is **Lactobacillus plantarum NU06**. It is a probiotic acting as an immunomodulatory agent and regulating the secretion of cytokines (cytokines modulate immune responses). This probiotic improves skin barrier function and has antimicrobial activity, promoting skin health and preventing acne.

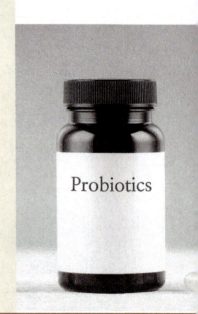

Topical Probiotics for Skin Health
Topical probiotics are recommended for treatment of acne, psoriasis, eczema, rosacea, fungal infections, athletes' foot, itchy skin and ringworm. Topical probiotics are available in spray or cream form.

- **Konjac glucomannan hydrolysates (GMH)** - there is the synbiotic ability of probiotic bacteria and konjac glucomannan hydrolysates (GMH) to inhibit acne-inducing bacterium, Cutibacterium acnes growth.

- **Fish Oil**
Fish oil contains omega-3 fatty acids and may improve inflammatory skin conditions like acne, by improving skin barrier function and regulating skin cell production and sebum levels, inhibiting inflammation from acne lesions and healing of acne scarring.

- **Marine Collagen**

The best form of collagen is powder form because it provides a significant dose of collagen peptides. The best kind of collagen powder for people with acne is marine collagen. Marine collagen is extracted from fish skin or scales and contains smaller particle sizes than other types of collagen, being absorbed better into the bloodstream. Types I and III of marine collagen are the most effective for promoting collagen production in the skin, nails and hair. Collagen helps to maintain the skin's hydration and elasticity.

Acne can cause scars. Collagen intake provides your body with the necessary amino acids for scar repair.

Marine Collagen improves skin health also thanks to healing the gut lining. If the gut lining is damaged, harmful toxins can get into the bloodstream, causing inflammation. Collagen improves the bacterial balance in the gut, promoting a healthier microbiome.

Inflammation is one of the key factors causing acne development. Marine collagen peptides can suppress inflammatory proteins such as IGF-1 and present immunomodulatory and antioxidant properties.

Collagen's amino acids help to balance our hormones, especially cortisol (a stress hormone) and oestrogen. Imbalances in cortisol and oestrogen levels can be involved in developing inflammation and skin issues. Moreover, the amino acid glycine helps the liver to eliminate toxins and excess hormones, restoring hormonal balance and improving gut and skin health.

Acne can cause scars. Collagen intake provides your body with the necessary amino acids for scar repair.

- **Vitamin C**

Vitamin C is an essential antioxidant that supports skin health in many ways, protecting against free radical damage that can accelerate ageing, boosting collagen production for skin elasticity and reducing inflammation.

Natural sources of vitamin C include citrus fruits, tomatoes, broccoli and peppers. Supplements containing vitamin C are also widely available.

- **Lecithin**

Lecithin is a mixture of fats that are essential to cells in the human body, including phospholipids, glycolipids and triglycerides. It can be found in many foods, including non-GMO soybeans, sunflower seeds and egg yolks.

Lecithin acts as an emollient, helping to moisturise the skin. Well-hydrated skin is less likely to experience acne. Lecithin also strengthens the skin's natural barrier, protecting against external irritants.

- **Zinc**

Zinc is a mineral that helps fight acne. You can take it as an oral supplement or use it as a topical treatment.

It is better to check your zinc level before oral supplementation (from blood or Elemental Hair Analysis) because excessive zinc intake can lead to a copper and iron deficiency. Consult a Functional Medicine Practitioner or other health practitioner on how much zinc to supplement.

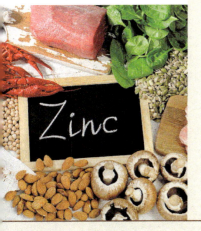

Using topical zinc treatment proves to be the safest.

Recent studies found that zinc can decrease oil production in the skin, battle acne-causing bacteria through antimicrobial activity, decrease inflammation and promote wound healing. Zinc deficiencies often coincide with inflammatory skin conditions.
The richest food sources of zinc include meat, fish and seafood. Other foods containing zinc are cashews and other nuts, pomegranate and pumpkin seeds.

- **Multivitamin ADEK**

Vitamin A
Vitamin A regulates sebum production, supports cell growth and immunity and reduces inflammation. All those factors are crucial for skin health.
Food sources include liver, fish oils, orange and yellow vegetables, like carrots and pumpkin. Acne patients may benefit from vitamin A supplementation, but only under medical supervision due to toxicity risks if over-consumed. You can also use vitamin A as a topical medication to fight acne. Most topical medications contain chemically altered vitamin A into a retinoid that you can apply to the skin. Retinoids provide effective treatment for acne because of their ability to heal the skin rapidly.

Vitamin D
Vitamin D is important for the immune system and may also help treat and prevent acne. This vitamin regulates skin cell production and decreases inflammation.
Natural sources include sunlight, fish and eggs, but many people are still deficient, especially in the winter months. That is why supplementation in most cases is necessary.

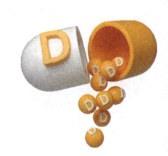

A 2021 study found that acne patients frequently had insufficient vitamin D levels. Supplementing this vitamin significantly decreased acne severity after 2 months of treatment.

Vitamin E
Vitamin E is an anti-inflammatory antioxidant that encourages healing acne scarring. Natural sources include nuts, avocados and spinach.

- **Silica**

Silica can reduce acne by enhancing collagen production, which ensures healthy external skin cell layers and by helping to remove the toxins we ingest from food. These toxins can enter the bloodstream, causing inflammation, which often leads to acne. Silica is also anti-inflammatory and can help relieve the symptoms of acne, psoriasis and eczema. Natural sources include green beans, bananas, leafy greens and lentils.

- **Green Tea Extract**

Green tea extract (GTE) helps treat and prevent acne breakouts. GTE contains polyphenol compounds called catechins that reduce excess sebum production. A 2017 study confirmed GTE can inhibit sebocytes, the oil-producing skin cells frequently overactive in the skin of acne patients.

- **Resveratrol**

Resveratrol is a polyphenol, which provides antioxidant protection to the skin. Resveratrol shows anti-inflammatory and antimicrobial effects and may help reduce acne breakouts and promote clearer skin.

Copyright©2025 Katarzyna Blochowiak This book is registered with **Protect My Work**

OTHER SUPPLEMENTS FOR HEALTHY SKIN

• **Ceramides**
Ceramides are lipids or fats that are found in skin cells. They are the building blocks of the skin and constitute 30% to 40% of your outer skin layer.
Ceramides play an essential role in water-retention function creating a barrier preventing the entry of germs into your body.

• **Caprylic acid**
Caprylic acid is one of the main fatty acids found in coconut oil and shows antibacterial, antiviral, antifungal, and anti-inflammatory properties. Caprylic acid can improve acne and reduce skin inflammation. Additionally, it has a beneficial effect on microbial balance in the gut, especially in eliminating dysbiotic yeast. It helps create a beneficial bacteria-friendly environment.

• **Maca Root**
Maca root is a plant native to Peru that may help balance your hormones and improve your mood. It can also enhance fitness performance and sexual health. The typical recommended dosage is 1,500 to 3,000 mg daily. Maca powder can be added to drinks like smoothies, mixed into vegan yogurt or used as an ingredient while baking.

• **Vitex agnus castus (Chasteberry)**
Vitex agnus castus (Chasteberry) is an herbal supplement that improves hormonal acne but it's not a remedy for all forms of female acne. It can help regain female hormonal balance by improving signalling from the pituitary gland. The pituitary gland makes, stores and releases hormones.

CAUTIONARY NOTICE
Vitex Agnus castus is for use in women over 18 years of age.

- **B Vitamins**

Low levels of B vitamins are linked to skin issues like acne, dermatitis and rashes. People with gut dysbiosis often are deficient in B vitamins.

Vitamin B1 (Thiamine) is essential for proper nerve functions and is called the "anti-stress vitamin." This vitamin supports both the immune and the nervous system, helping prevent stress-related breakouts.

Vitamin B2 (Riboflavin) supports collagen maintenance and reduces inflammation. It also regulates mucus secretion in the skin, preventing the dryness that cause excessive oil production leading to acne. Vitamin B2 improves also zinc absorption, which is an important mineral for skin health.

Studies show that **Vitamin B3 (niacinamide)** can repair skin, reduce redness and inflammation, minimise pore appearance and control excess sebum production within follicles.

Vitamin B5 (pantothenic acid) can help normalise oil gland function. 2014 study found that supplementing vitamin B5 significantly reduced oil production, facial lesions and inflammation in acne patients after just 12 weeks.

Vitamin B6 is important for modulating oestrogen and testosterone levels. Studies show that B6

supplementation regulates hormones and reduces premenstrual acne.

CAUTIONARY NOTICE
Dr. Li discovered that supplementation of vitamin B12 can increase the amount of that vitamin on facial skin which causes Cutibacterium acnes to produce more of something called porphyrins, which results in inflammation. This process could lead to acne. So be careful with B12 supplementation during acne treatment.

- **Magnesium**

Magnesium is a mineral that may improve inflammatory skin disorders. Magnesium has a calming effect on the nervous system and may reduce sebum production and inflammation.
Maintaining adequate magnesium levels supports healthy skin function. Dietary sources include nuts, seeds, leafy greens and legumes.

- **Selenium**

Some studies show selenium deficiency links to skin damage and disorders.
Selenium is a trace mineral regulating oxidative stress response within the body and playing a key role in the antioxidant enzyme glutathione production, which protects skin cells from free radicals and damage.
Dietary sources include Brazil nuts, seafood, eggs, meat, seeds and mushrooms. Quality supplements are widely available as well, but overdosing could cause side effects. Symptoms of selenium toxicity include nausea, vomiting, hair loss, fatigue, irritability, nail discolouration, brittleness and foul breath odour.

CHAPTER FOURTEEN SUMMARY
SUPPLEMENTS FOR HEALTHY SKIN

There are many natural substances, including vitamins, minerals, and plant extracts that are very effective in fighting acne and improving your skin health.

The response to herbal treatments may vary, and what works for one person may not be effective for another. It is recommended to consult a healthcare practitioner before choosing natural remedies, to ensure what is best for your skin condition and overall health.

FIRST CHOICE SUPPLEMENTS FOR HEALTHY SKIN

multi-strain probiotics
Konjac glucomannan hydrolysates (GMH)
Fish Oil
Marine Collagen
Vitamin C
Lecithin
Zinc
Multivitamin ADEK
Silica
Green Tea Extract
Resveratrol

OTHER SUPPLEMENTS FOR HEALTHY SKIN

Ceramides
Caprylic acid
Maca Root
Vitex agnus castus (Chasteberry)
B-Vitamins
Magnesium
Selenium

CHAPTER FIFTEEN

NATURAL COSMETICS FOR ACNE

BELOW YOU CAN FIND THE MOST IMPORTANT INGREDIENTS OF NATURAL COSMETICS FOR ACNE.

Many cosmetics contain a few of those ingredients, to work more effectively.

Always choose natural, toxin-free beauty products.
It is recommended to contact a health practitioner to consult which product will work best for you.

FIRST CHOICE NATURAL COSMETICS FOR ACNE

- **Activated charcoal**

Activated charcoal can reduce the buildup of oil and prevent acne and breakouts.

Charcoal is made from materials like coconut or nutshells. Activated charcoal is produced by heating charcoal in the presence of a gas. This process causes the charcoal to develop lots of pores that trap chemicals, impurities and oil. Activated charcoal shows anti-inflammatory and anti-bacterial properties, which means it can reduce acne and prevent forming of new spots.
Activated charcoal may help improve the texture of skin and unclog pores by binding to toxins and bacteria. It can remove dead skin cells and blackheads too. Activated charcoal reduces the appearance of enlarged pores.

You can find this ingredient in exfoliators, cleansers, soaps and face masks.

- **Topical zinc**

Zinc has anti-inflammatory properties and can fight bacteria causing acne. This mineral may also help to relieve redness and irritation associated with moderate-to-severe acne and even reduce the appearance of acne scars. A recent studies found that zinc can decrease oil production in the skin, fight inflammation and promote wound healing. Zinc deficiencies often coincide with inflammatory skin conditions.

Topical lotions and creams containing zinc can help improve acne. Using topical zinc twice a day should show a decrease in acne within 2 weeks.

- **Hyaluronic acid**

Applied topically hyaluronic acid, retains moisture, providing optimal hydration levels in the skin. Proper skin hydration is essential for acne patients to prevent excessive dryness and irritation that can worsen breakouts. Hyaluronic acid also helps repair skin by enhancing collagen synthesis and improving skin texture. It also is beneficial in treating acne scars, as hydrated skin recovers more effectively.
Hyaluronic acid is used in moisturising creams, lotions, ointments and serums.

•Topical Niacinamide

Topical niacinamide helps treat some skin conditions, like acne and eczema. This vitamin helps the skin build proteins and lock in moisture to prevent the damaging effects of external factors.
Niacinamide builds skin immunity. The components of niacinamide are helpful in restoring the cellular energy of the skin's cells and repair damaged DNA.
This vitamin also reduces the immunosuppressive effects of the sun's UV rays, preventing skin degeneration and it's premature ageing.
There are serums and creams with niacinamide available on the market.

• Green tea (Camellia sinensis) extract

Green tea extract has also demonstrated effectiveness in treating acne, presenting antiseptic and anti-inflammatory effects. One study showed that a 2% lotion of green tea applied topically during six weeks among 20 proved patients improved their skin.

Catechins are the dominant polyphenols in green tea. The catechins in topical green tea extract preparations decrease inflammation and fight the bacteria involved in acne development and scarring. This product also reduces sebum excretions in the skin.

Green tea extract is an effective topical therapy for acne of all severities. There are serums, lotions and creams available that contain green tea extract.

• **Aloe Vera**

Aloe Vera gel shows antibacterial, anti-inflammatory effects and promotes wound healing. Some studies suggested that Aloe Vera gel treatment is effective in reducing non-inflammatory and inflammatory acne lesions.

One study published in 2021 innovatively utilised ultrasound, which enhanced the absorption of aloe vera gel. This scientific evidence suggests that this new therapy significantly improved acne. Aloe vera demonstrates anti-acne and anti-inflammatory properties, helping to reduce redness and general inflammation. Moreover, aloe vera contains six antiseptic agents that fight many different microorganisms, including bacteria, fungi and viruses.

There are many Aloe Vera cosmetic products, like cleansers, gels, serums, lotions and creams.
It is important to note that Aloe Vera's effectiveness can vary among individuals.

OTHER NATURAL COSMETICS FOR ACNE

- **Ceramides**

Ceramides are lipids or fats found in skin cells and make up 30% to 40% of the outer skin layer. Ceramides play a key role in water-retention function and preventing the entry of germs into your body.
They are present in many skin care products, like ceramide serums, moisturizers, creams and toners.

- **Witch hazel**

Witch hazel has anti-inflammatory and astringent properties, helping to fight acne. It can soothe the skin, as well as absorb and remove excess sebum.
Witch hazel contains water-soluble polyphenols called tannins, which can kill bacteria associated with acne, Cutibacterium acnes (C. acnes). This plant constricts blood vessels minimising the appearance of red, irritated skin and can reduce skin swelling.

- **Honeysuckle**

Honeysuckle demonstrates antibacterial properties, reducing the growth of acne-causing bacteria. It can also act as a gentle astringent, helping to tone the skin and minimising the appearance of enlarged pores.
Honeysuckle also has anti-inflammatory properties that can reduce skin irritation.

- **Marigold (Calendula officinalis)**

Calendula officinalis, commonly known as marigold, has been used for a long time in dermatology for conditions such as redness, acne, minor burns and fungal infections.

- **Chrysanthemum morifolium**

Chrysanthemum morifolium is a well-known traditional Chinese herb, that has been proven to have a certain inhibitory effect on bacteria strains causing acne. The study from 2022 suggested that the oils from different flowering stages and non-medicinal parts of Chrysanthemum morifolium have antibacterial activity against Staphylococcus aureus and Cutibacterium acnes and they can be effective ingredients of anti-inflammatory and acne cosmetics.

- **English walnut (Juglans regia) and Common guava (Psidium guajava)**

English walnut (Juglans regia) and Common guava (Psidium guajava) leaf extracts are also effective in treating acne due to their anti-inflammatory and antimicrobial properties. The extracts of these plants fight bacteria and inflammation, reducing acne.

- **Rosemary gel (Rosmarinus officinalis)**

One study showed Rosemary gel promising results in significantly improving acne vulgaris symptoms. This suggests that rosemary has the potential to be an alternative treatment for acne patients looking for natural remedies.

- **Scutellaria Baicalensis (Baikal Skullcap)**

Scutellaria Baicalensis extract shows strong anti-inflammatory properties and can be used for various skin conditions, including acne, eczema and psoriasis. This herb can reduce inflammation and soothe irritated skin.

- **Centella Asiatica (Gotu Kola)**

Centella Asiatica (Gotu Kola) shows strong anti-inflammatory and wound-healing properties and can be beneficial for acne patients, calming irritated or inflamed skin, helping to soothe the skin and healing blemishes. It can also be helpful for conditions like eczema and psoriasis.

CHAPTER FIFTEEN SUMMARY

NATURAL COSMETICS FOR ACNE

Below you can find the most important ingredients of natural cosmetics for acne. Many cosmetics contain a few of those ingredients, to work more effectively.

FIRST CHOICE NATURAL COSMETICS FOR ACNE

- Activated charcoal
- Topical zinc
- Hyaluronic acid
- Topical Niacinamide
- Green tea (Camellia sinensis) extract
- Aloe Vera

OTHER NATURAL COSMETICS FOR ACNE

- Ceramides
- Witch hazel
- Honeysuckle
- Chrysanthemum morifolium
- Marigold (Calendula officinalis)
- English walnut (Juglans regia) and Common guava (Psidium guajava)
- Rosemary gel (Rosmarinus officinalis)
- Scutellaria Baicalensis (Baikal Skullcap)
- Centella Asiatica (Gotu Kola)

CHAPTER SIXTEEN

ALTERNATIVE ACNE THERAPIES

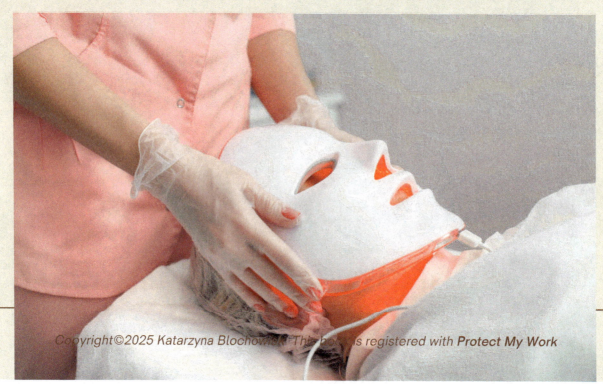

16.1. LIGHT THERAPY (PHOTOTHERAPY)

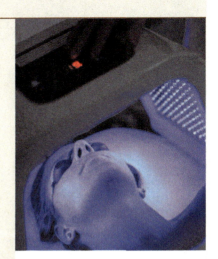

Light Therapy for Acne is becoming more popular. There are home-use LED masks available. In-office treatment is also an option.
Studies show that the best efficacy of light therapies for acne is for blue and blue-red light. Phototherapy is the most effective on mild to moderate acne lesions, especially for acne caused by inflammation or bacteria. Light-based therapy is a safe and effective treatment option for inflammatory acne vulgaris. The effects of light therapy are comparable to the effects of oral antibiotics but work faster and with fewer side effects.

Blue light therapy

Blue light therapy is an effective treatment to fight acne breakouts.
The wavelength of blue light has an antimicrobial effect, killing many types of bacteria that can colonise your pores and oil glands, causing breakouts. Blue light therapy has anti-inflammatory properties, decreasing symptoms of skin disorders like acne and redness.

Red light therapy

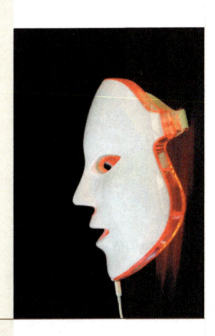

Red light therapy doesn't show the same antibacterial properties as blue light therapy but is also effective for acne and demonstrates anti-inflammatory capabilities. Red light therapy has healing effects and can reduce the visibility of acne scarring. This type of light therapy reaches deeper layers of your skin to repair tissue. In the case of acne caused by a chronic skin condition, red light therapy is the best light therapy option for you.

Infrared light

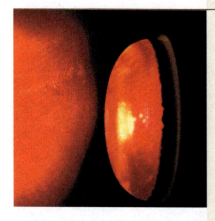

Infrared therapy is an innovative light therapy to treat pain and inflammation in various parts of the body. Infrared light is an approved type of light therapy to treat pimples, including those that develop on the back. Infrared light cannot treat blackheads, whiteheads, nodules or cysts.

CAUTIONARY NOTICE
Some people should avoid light therapy, especially those on antibiotic therapy, those extremely sensitive to sunlight, and pregnant women.

16.2. PHOTOPNEUMATIC THERAPY

Photopneumatic therapy combines an intense pulsed light (IPL) laser with a gentle vacuum to fight acne by cleansing pores, killing bacteria and purifying the skin. This vacuum suction removes dead cells, impurities and excess oil from the pores, while an intense pulsed light (IPL) laser kills Cutibacterium acnes bacteria associated with acne breakouts. This therapy cannot treat acne nodules or cysts.

Laser treatment reduces oil gland activity and sebaceous gland secretions without serious side effects. Swelling and redness are common after lasers and light treatments, but these are usually mild and disappear within a few hours.

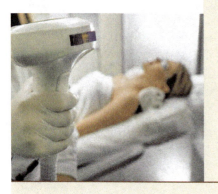

16.3. EXFOLIATING FACIAL TREATMENTS

Exfoliating facial treatments are well known and offer some benefits for acne patients, including unclogging pores, minimizing acne and stimulating the production of collagen.

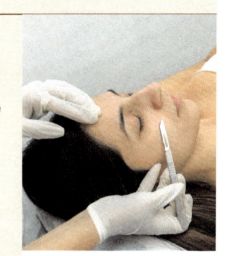

There are 3 types of exfoliating facial treatments:

1. Dermaplaning

Dermaplaning uses a scalpel-like tool to remove the dead cells and unclog pores, preventing acne. Dermaplaning smooths skin texture, minimizes acne scars and improves hyperpigmentation and skin tone.

2. Hydrafacial

Hydrafacial is professional exfoliating facial treatment, also known as the Red Carpet Facial because of its popularity among celebrities.

A HydraFacial is a patented skin treatment available in dermatology offices. It is three-step process, that consists of deep-cleaning, exfoliating and hydration your skin. This therapy can improve many skin conditions, including acne, dryness and wrinkles.
Hydrafacial uses the combination of special serums and technology to cleanse and hydrates the skin. HydraFacial serum is made of peptides, antioxidants and hyaluronic acid that nourish and hydrate the skin.

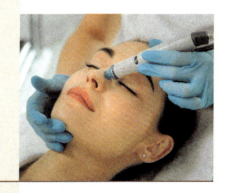

3. VI Peel

VI Peel® is a chemical peel that can be used to improve a variety of skin conditions. This facial treatment uses an acidic solution to remove the outer layers of skin and stimulate the production of new skin cells. It can be performed on the face and neck.

VI Peel can improve tone and texture of the skin; minimize acne scarring and reduce the post inflammatory hyperpigmentation caused by acne.

CHAPTER SIXTEEN SUMMARY

ALTERNATIVE ACNE THERAPIES

16.1. Light Therapy for Acne (phototherapy)

Light Therapy for Acne is becoming more popular. There are home-use LED masks available. In-office treatment is also an option.
Studies show that the best efficacy of light therapies for acne is for blue and blue-red light.

Types of light therapy

- Blue light therapy
- Red light therapy
- Infrared light

16.2. Photopneumatic therapy

Photopneumatic therapy combines an intense pulsed light (IPL) laser with a gentle vacuum to fight acne by cleansing pores, killing bacteria and purifying the skin.

16.3. 3 Types of Exfoliating Facial Treatments

1. Dermaplaning

Dermaplaning uses a scalpel-like tool to remove the dead cells and unclog pores. This therapy minimizes acne scars as well as improves hyperpigmentation.

2. Hydrafacial

Hydrafacial uses a combination of special serums and technology to cleanse and hydrate the skin. HydraFacial serum is made of peptides, antioxidants and hyaluronic acid that nourish and hydrate the skin.

3. VI Peel

VI Peel® is a chemical peel used to remove the outer layers of skin and stimulate the production of new skin cells. VI Peel can improve the tone and texture of the skin; minimise acne scarring and reduce the post-inflammatory hyperpigmentation caused by acne.

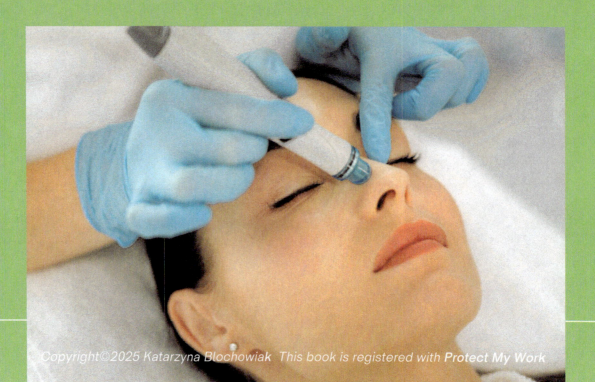

CHAPTER SEVENTEEN

ACNE DIAGNOSTICS

THERE ARE A FEW TESTS THAT CAN BE USEFUL FOR ACNE:

1) Comprehensive Stool Analysis with Parasitology

2) Food Intolerance Testing IgG or Alcat Test

3) Zinc level (blood plasma or urine test or Elemental Hair Analysis)

4) Vitamin D level (blood plasma)

5) Celiac disease- IgA (antibodies), HLA DQ2, and DQ8 (genetic test)

6) Heavy metals test (Elemental Hair Analysis, Heavy Metal Blood Test, or urine test).

Elemental Hair Analysis test detects not only levels of toxic metals but also "good" minerals like magnesium, potassium, selenium and zinc.

CHAPTER EIGHTEEN

EPILOGUE

Our journey towards healthy skin is ending here. I hope you enjoyed it and found many inspiring, life-changing information! I promise it will not only change the look of your skin but improve your overall health and prevent other health problems! All information provided is based on scientific evidence.

Many used those little steps while aiming for healthy skin and now enjoy an acne-free life!

So say the last word to acne and Hello to your new-healthy looking skin!

Katarzyna Blochowiak
Certified Functional Medicine Practitioner, Nutritionist

www.diet-designer.com
contact@diet-designer.com

BIBLIOGRAPHY

1) Karolina Chilicka, Iwona Dzieńdziora-Urbińska, Renata Szyguła, Binnaz Asanova, and Danuta Nowicka. Enzo Berardesca, Academic Editor
Microbiome and Probiotics in Acne Vulgaris—A Narrative Review
Life (Basel). 2022 Mar; 12(3): 422. Published online 2022 Mar 15.
https://www.ncbi.nlm.nih.gov/pmc/articles/PMC8953587/

2) Bickers DR, Lim HW, Margolis D, Weinstock MA, Goodman C, Faulkner E et al.
The burden of skin diseases
2004 a joint project of the American Academy of Dermatology Association and the Society for Investigative Dermatology. Journal of the American Academy of Dermatology 2006;55:490-500.

3) Bhate K, Williams HC. Epidemiology of acne vulgaris. The British journal of dermatology 2013;168:474-85.

4) Holzmann R , Shakery K. Postadolescent acne in females. Skin pharmacology and physiology 2014;27 Suppl 1:3-8.

5) Khunger N , Kumar C. A clinico-epidemiological study of adult acne: is it different from adolescent acne? Indian journal of dermatology, venereology and leprology 2012;78:335-41.

6) Tanghetti EA, Kawata AK, Daniels SR, Yeomans K, Burk CT , Callender VD. Understanding the Burden of Adult Female Acne. The Journal of Clinical and Aesthetic Dermatology 2014;7:22-30.

7) Pedro Sánchez-Pellicer, Laura Navarro-Moratalla, Eva Núñez-Delegido, Beatriz Ruzafa-Costas, Juan Agüera-Santos and Vicente Navarro-López
Acne, Microbiome, and Probiotics: The Gut-Skin Axis
MiBioPath Research Group, Department of Clinical Medicine, Health Sciences Faculty, Catholic University of Murcia, Campus de los Jerónimos 135, 30107 Murcia, Spain
Infectious Diseases Unit, University Hospital of Vinalopó, Carrer Tonico Sansano Mora 14, 03293 Elche, Spain, Microorganisms 2022, 10(7), 1303;
https://www.mdpi.com/2076-2607/10/7/1303

8) Nazik H Hasrat and Asaad Q Al-Yassen, The Relationship Between Acne Vulgaris and Insulin Resistance
Monitoring Editor: Alexander Muacevic and John R Adler
Cureus. 2023 Jan; 15(1): e34241. Published online 2023 Jan 26
https://www.ncbi.nlm.nih.gov/pmc/articles/PMC9964714/

9) Tânia Nascimento, Diana Gomes, Ricardo Simões, and Maria da Graça Miguel
Tea Tree Oil: Properties and the Therapeutic Approach to Acne—A Review
Simona Gabriela Bungau, Academic Editor
Antioxidants (Basel). 2023 Jun; 12(6): 1264. Published online 2023 Jun 12
https://www.ncbi.nlm.nih.gov/pmc/articles/PMC10295805/

10) Azadeh Goodarzi, Samaneh Mozafarpoor, Mohammad Bodaghabadi, Masoumeh Mohamadi
The potential of probiotics for treating acne vulgaris: A review of literature on acne and microbiota Dermatol Ther. 2020 May;33(3):e13279. Epub 2020 Apr 7.
https://pubmed.ncbi.nlm.nih.gov/32266790/

11) Young Bok Lee, Eun Jung Byun, and Hei Sung Kim
Potential Role of the Microbiome in Acne: A Comprehensive Review
J Clin Med. 2019 Jul; 8(7): 987. Published online 2019 Jul 7.
https://www.ncbi.nlm.nih.gov/pmc/articles/PMC6678709/

12) Paul Macklis, MS, Kevin Adams, BA, Jessica Kaffenberger, MD, Purnima Kumar, BDS MS PhD, Andrew Krispinsky, MD, and Benjamin Kaffenberger, MD
The Association Between Oral Health and Skin Disease
J Clin Aesthet Dermatol. 2020 Jun; 13(6): 48-53. Published online 2020 Jun 1.
https://www.ncbi.nlm.nih.gov/pmc/articles/PMC7442307/

13) Kober, M. and Bowe, W. (2015).
The effect of probiotics on immune regulation, acne, and photoaging.
International Journal of Women's Dermatology, [online] 1(2), pp.85-89.

14) Delost, G., Delost, M., Armile, J. and Lloyd, J. (2016).
Staphylococcus aureus carriage rates and antibiotic resistance patterns in patients with acne vulgaris.
Journal of the American Academy of Dermatology, [online] 74(4), pp.673-678.

15) Teotia, U., Kumar, R., Mishra, A., Verma, D.,
Role of Probiotics and probiotic beverages on human health.
International Journal of Pharmaceutical and Medicinal Research, [online] 2(3), pp.78-84.

16) Deng, Y., Wang, H., Zhou, J., Mou, Y., Wang, G. and Xiong, X. (2018).
Patients with Acne Vulgaris Have a Distinct Gut Microbiota in Comparison with Healthy Controls.
Acta Dermato Venereologica, 98(8), pp.783-790.
https://www.ncbi.nlm.nih.gov/pmc/articles/PMC8070017/

17) Agnieszka Daca and Tomasz Jarzembowski
From the Friend to the Foe—Enterococcus faecalis Diverse Impact on the Human Immune System
Int J Mol Sci. 2024 Feb; 25(4): 2422. Published online 2024 Feb 19.
https://www.ncbi.nlm.nih.gov/pmc/articles/PMC10888668/

18) Hye Sung Han, Sun Hye Shin, Bo-Yun Choi, Nayeon Koo, Sanghyun Lim, Dooheon Son, Myung Jun Chung , Kui Young Park , Woo Jun Sul
A split face study on the effect of an anti-acne product containing fermentation products of Enterococcus faecalis CBT SL-5 on skin microbiome modification and acne improvement.
Randomized Controlled Trial J Microbiol. 2022 May;60(5):488-495. Epub 2022 Mar 14.
https://pubmed.ncbi.nlm.nih.gov/35286606/

19) Vito Chiantera, Antonio Simone Laganà, Sabrina Basciani, Maurizio Nordio, and Mariano Bizzarri Jessica Mandrioli, Academic Editor
A Critical Perspective on the Supplementation of Akkermansia muciniphila: Benefits and Harms
Life (Basel). 2023 Jun; 13(6): 1247. Published online 2023 May 24.
https://www.ncbi.nlm.nih.gov/pmc/articles/PMC10301191/

20) Macpherson AJ, Slack E. The functional interactions of commensal bacteria with intestinal secretory IgA.
Curr Opin Gastroenterol. 2007 Nov;23(6):673-8.

21) Andrea Michielan and Renata D'Incà Intestinal Permeability in Inflammatory Bowel Disease: Pathogenesis, Clinical Evaluation, and Therapy of Leaky Gut
Mediators Inflamm. 2015; 2015: 628157. Published online 2015 Oct 25.
https://www.ncbi.nlm.nih.gov/pmc/articles/PMC4637104/

22) Qianru Chen, Oliver Chen, Isabela M Martins, Hu Hou, Xue Zhao, Jeffrey B Blumberg, Bafang Li Collagen peptides ameliorate intestinal epithelial barrier dysfunction in immunostimulatory Caco-2 cell monolayers via enhancing tight junctions.
Food Funct. 2017 Mar 22;8(3):1144-1151
https://pubmed.ncbi.nlm.nih.gov/28174772/

23) Benjamin Seethaler, Katja Lehnert, Maryam Yahiaoui-Doktor, Maryam Basrai, Walter Vetter, Marion Kiechle & Stephan C. Bischoff
Omega-3 polyunsaturated fatty acids improve intestinal barrier integrity—albeit to a lesser degree than short-chain fatty acids: an exploratory analysis of the randomized controlled LIBRE trial.
Eur J Nutr 62, 2779-2791 (2023). Published: 15 June 2023. Volume 62, pages 2779-2791, (2023)
https://link.springer.com/article/10.1007/s00394-023-03172-
2#:~:text=Using%20bi%2D%20and%20multivariate%20analyses,were%20associated%20with%20barrier%20d
ysfunction.

24) Andrea Michielan and Renata D'Incà
Intestinal Permeability in Inflammatory Bowel Disease: Pathogenesis, Clinical Evaluation, and Therapy of Leaky Gut
Mediators Inflamm. 2015; 2015: 628157. Published online 2015 Oct 25.
https://www.ncbi.nlm.nih.gov/pmc/articles/PMC4637104/

25) Svenja Plöger, Friederike Stumpff, Gregory B Penner, Jörg-Dieter Schulzke, Gotthold Gäbel, Holger Martens, Zanming Shen, Dorothee Günzel, Joerg R Aschenbach
Microbial butyrate and its role for barrier function in the gastrointestinal tract.
Ann N Y Acad Sci. 2012 Jul:1258:52-9.
https://pubmed.ncbi.nlm.nih.gov/22731715/

26) Bin Wang, Guoyao Wu, Zhigang Zhou, Zhaolai Dai, Yuli Sun, Yun Ji, Wei Li, Weiwei Wang, Chuang Liu , Feng Han , Zhenlong Wu
Glutamine and intestinal barrier function.
Amino Acids. 2015 Oct;47(10):2143-54. Epub 2014 Jun 26.
https://pubmed.ncbi.nlm.nih.gov/24965526/

27) Bodo C Melnik Linking diet to acne metabolomics, inflammation, and comedogenesis: an update
Clin Cosmet Investig Dermatol. 2015 Jul 15:8:371-88. doi: 10.2147/CCID.S69135. eCollection 2015. https://pubmed.ncbi.nlm.nih.gov/26203267/

28) Aslı Aksu Çerman MD, Ezgi Aktaş MD, İlknur Kıvanç Altunay MD, Janset Erkul Arıcı MD, Aysın Tulunay PhD, Feyza Yener Ozturk MD
Dietary glycemic factors, insulin resistance, and adiponectin levels in acne vulgaris.
Journal of the American Academy of Dermatology. Volume 75, Issue 1, July 2016, Pages 155-162
https://www.sciencedirect.com/science/article/abs/pii/S0190962216014857

29) Huarui Lu and Haojie Huang FOXO1: A potential target for human diseases
Curr Drug Targets. Author manuscript; available in PMC 2015 Oct 1.
Published in final edited form as:Curr Drug Targets. 2011 Aug; 12(9): 1235-1244.
https://www.ncbi.nlm.nih.gov/pmc/articles/PMC4591039/

30) L Tasli, S Turgut, N Kacar, C Ayada, M Coban, R Akcilar, S Ergin
Insulin-like growth factor-I gene polymorphism in acne vulgaris.
J Eur Acad Dermatol Venereol. 2013 Feb;27(2):254-7.
https://pubmed.ncbi.nlm.nih.gov/23457723/

31) S Vora, A Ovhal, H Jerajani, N Nair, A Chakrabortty
Correlation of facial sebum to serum insulin-like growth factor-1 in patients with acne.
Br J Dermatol. 2008 Sep;159(4):990-1. Epub 2008 Jul 24.
https://pubmed.ncbi.nlm.nih.gov/18652583/

32) Benjamin Lebwohl, Jonas Söderling, Bjorn Roelstraete, Mark G Lebwohl, Peter H R Green, Jonas F Ludvigsson
Risk of skin disorders in patients with celiac disease: A population-based cohort study.
J Am Acad Dermatol. 2021 Dec;85(6):1456-1464. doi: 10.1016/j.jaad.2020.10.079. Epub 2020 Nov 1. https://pubmed.ncbi.nlm.nih.gov/33144153/

33) Tariq Mahmood, Naveed Akhtar, Barkat Ali Khan, Haji M Shoaib Khan, Tariq Saeed
Outcomes of 3% green tea emulsion on skin sebum production in male volunteers.
Bosn J Basic Med Sci. 2010 Aug;10(3):260-4.
https://pubmed.ncbi.nlm.nih.gov/20846135/

34) Golandam Khayef, Julia Young, Bonny Burns-Whitmore, Thomas Spalding
Effects of fish oil supplementation on inflammatory acne.
Lipids Health Dis. 2012 Dec 3:11:165.
https://pubmed.ncbi.nlm.nih.gov/23206895/

35) Keisuke Nakase, Misato Momose, Tomoko Yukawa, and Hidemasa Nakaminami
Development of skin sebum medium and inhibition of lipase activity in Cutibacterium acnes by oleic acid.
Access Microbiol. 2022; 4(10): acmi000397.
Published online 2022 Oct 3.
https://www.ncbi.nlm.nih.gov/pmc/articles/PMC9675171/

36) Nazan Emiroğlu, Fatma Pelin Cengiz, Funda Kemeriz
Insulin resistance in severe acne vulgaris.
Postepy Dermatol Alergol. 2015 Aug;32(4):281-5. Epub 2015 Aug 12.
https://pubmed.ncbi.nlm.nih.gov/26366152/

37) Alexander Bertuccioli, Marco Gervasi, Giosuè Annibalini, Beatrice Binato, Fabrizio Perroni, Marco B. L. Rocchi, Davide Sisti,corresponding author and Stefano Amatori
Use of Streptococcus salivarius K12 in supporting the mucosal immune function of active young subjects: A randomised double-blind study.
https://www.ncbi.nlm.nih.gov/pmc/articles/PMC10019894/

38) Staci Brandt The clinical effects of zinc as a topical or oral agent on the clinical response and pathophysiologic mechanisms of acne: a systematic review of the literature.
J Drugs Dermatol. 2013 May;12(5):542-5.
https://pubmed.ncbi.nlm.nih.gov/23652948/

39) Yong-Guy Kim, Jin-Hyung Lee, Sunyoung Park, Jintae Lee
The Anticancer Agent 3,3'-Diindolylmethane Inhibits Multispecies Biofilm Formation by Acne-Causing Bacteria and Candida albicans
Microbiol Spectr. 2022 Feb 23;10(1):e0205621. Epub 2022 Feb 2.
https://pubmed.ncbi.nlm.nih.gov/35107361/

40) Michael Yang, Betsy Moclair, Virgil Hatcher, Jed Kaminetsky, Maria Mekas, Anne Chapas, and Jillian Capodice
A Randomized, Double-Blind, Placebo-Controlled Study of a Novel Pantothenic Acid-Based Dietary Supplement in Subjects with Mild to Moderate Facial Acne.
Dermatol Ther (Heidelb). 2014 Jun; 4(1): 93-101. Published online 2014 May 16
https://www.ncbi.nlm.nih.gov/pmc/articles/PMC4065280/

41) Elham Ebrahimi, Shiva Khayati Motlagh, Sima Nemati, and Zohreh Tavakoli
Effects of Magnesium and Vitamin B6 on the Severity of Premenstrual Syndrome Symptoms.
J Caring Sci. 2012 Dec; 1(4): 183-189. Published online 2012 Nov 22.
https://www.ncbi.nlm.nih.gov/pmc/articles/PMC4161081/

42) Mrinal Gupta, Vikram K. Mahajan, Karaninder S. Mehta, and Pushpinder S. Chauhan
Zinc Therapy in Dermatology: A Review.
Dermatol Res Pract. 2014; 2014: 709152. Published online 2014 Jul 10.
https://www.ncbi.nlm.nih.gov/pmc/articles/PMC4120804/

43) Hamid Nasri, Mahmoud Bahmani, Najmeh Shahinfard, Atefeh Moradi Nafchi, Shirin Saberianpour, and Mahmoud Rafieian Kopaei
Medicinal Plants for the Treatment of Acne Vulgaris: A Review of Recent Evidences.
Jundishapur J Microbiol. Ibid. 2015 Nov; 8(11): e25580. Published online 2015 Nov 21.
https://www.ncbi.nlm.nih.gov/pmc/articles/PMC4740760/

44) Therdpong Tempark M.D., Andrew Shem M.D., MSc, Suparuj Lueangarun M.D., MSc
Efficacy of ceramides and niacinamide-containing moisturizer versus hydrophilic cream in combination with topical anti-acne treatment in mild to moderate acne vulgaris: A split face, double-blinded, randomized controlled trial.
First published: 01 February 2024
https://onlinelibrary.wiley.com/doi/full/10.1111/jocd.16212

45) Philip D. Shenefelt. Herbal Treatment for Dermatologic Disorders
Herbal Medicine: Biomolecular and Clinical Aspects. 2nd edition.Benzie IFF, Wachtel-Galor S, editors. Boca Raton (FL): CRC Press/Taylor & Francis; 2011.
https://www.ncbi.nlm.nih.gov/books/NBK92761/

46) Xia-Jin Liu, Yi Li, Shu-Lan Su, Dan-Dan Wei, Hui Yan, Sheng Guo, Er-Xin Shang, Xiao-Dong Sun, and Jin-Ao Duan
Comparative Analysis of Chemical Composition andAntibacterial and Anti-Inflammatory Activities of theEssential Oils from Chrysanthemum morifolium ofDifferent Flowering Stages and Different Parts
Evid Based Complement Alternat Med. 2022; 2022: 5954963.
Published online 2022 Jun 6.
https://www.ncbi.nlm.nih.gov/pmc/articles/PMC9192287/

47) Supreet Jain, Nirav Rathod, Ravleen Nagi,corresponding author Jaideep Sur, Afshan Laheji, Naveen Gupta, Priyanka Agrawal, and Swati Prasad
Antibacterial Effect of Aloe Vera Gel against Oral Pathogens: An In-vitro Study
J Clin Diagn Res. 2016 Nov; 10(11): ZC41-ZC44. Published online 2016 Nov 1.
https://www.ncbi.nlm.nih.gov/pmc/articles/PMC5198455/

48) Hongyu Zhong, Xiang Li, Wanqi Zhang, Xiaoxiao Shen, Yuangang Lu, and Hongli Li
Efficacy of a New Non-drug Acne Therapy: Aloe Vera Gel Combined With Ultrasound and Soft Mask for the Treatment of Mild to Severe Facial Acne.
Front Med (Lausanne). 2021; 8: 662640. Published online 2021 May 21.
https://www.ncbi.nlm.nih.gov/pmc/articles/PMC8175793/

49) Mur, R., et al. Concentration of Antioxidant Compounds from Calendula officinalis through Sustainable Supercritical Technologies, and Computational Study of Their Permeability in Skin for Cosmetic Use.
Antioxidants (Basel). 2021, December 30.
https://pubmed.ncbi.nlm.nih.gov/35052598/

50) Qadan, F., et al. The antimicrobial activities of Psidium guajava and Juglans regia leaf extracts to acne-developing organisms. Am J Chin Med. 2005, n.d.
https://pubmed.ncbi.nlm.nih.gov/15974479/

51) Masoud, F., et al. The novel topical herbal gel might be an alternative treatment in patients with acne vulgaris: A randomized, double-blind controlled study. Phytomedicine Plus. May 2022.
https://www.sciencedirect.com/science/article/pii/S2667031322000185

51) Masoud, F., et al. The novel topical herbal gel might be an alternative treatment in patients with acne vulgaris: A randomized, double-blind controlled study. Phytomedicine Plus. May 2022. https://www.sciencedirect.com/science/article/pii/S2667031322000185

52) Susan Pei, Arun C. Inamadar, Keshavmurthy A. Adya, and Maria M. Tsoukas
Light-based therapies in acne treatment.
Indian Dermatol Online J. 2015 May-Jun; 6(3): 145-157.
https://www.ncbi.nlm.nih.gov/pmc/articles/PMC4439741/

53) Monica Elman, Joseph Lebzelter Light therapy in the treatment of acne vulgaris.
Dermatol Surg. 2004 Feb;30(2 Pt 1):139-46.
https://pubmed.ncbi.nlm.nih.gov/14756640/

54) Tianhong Dai, Asheesh Gupta, Clinton K. Murray, Mark S. Vrahas, George P. Tegos, and Michael R. Hamblin. Blue light for infectious diseases: Propionibacterium acnes, Helicobacter pylori, and beyond? Drug Resist Updat. 2012 Aug; 15(4): 223-236. Published online 2012 Jul

28.https://www.ncbi.nlm.nih.gov/pmc/articles/PMC3438385/

55) Handler, MZ, Bloom BS, et al. Energy-based devices in treatment of acne vulgaris. Dermatol Surg. 2016 May;42(5):573-85.

56) Nestor MS, Swenson N, et al. Physical modalities (devices) in the management of acne. Dermatol Clin. 2016 Apr;34(2):215-23.

57) Zaenglein AL, Pathy AL, et al. Guidelines of care for the management of acne vulgaris. J Am Acad Dermatol 2016 May;74(5):945-973.

58) Vicente Navarro-López, Eva Núñez-Delegido, Beatriz Ruzafa-Costas, Pedro Sánchez-Pellicer, Juan Agüera-Santos, and Laura Navarro-Moratalla Probiotics in the Therapeutic Arsenal of Dermatologists
Microorganisms. 2021 Jul; 9(7): 1513. Published online 2021 Jul 15.
https://www.ncbi.nlm.nih.gov/pmc/articles/PMC8303240/

59) Mamta Kaushik , Pallavi Reddy, Roshni Sharma, Pooja Udameshi, Neha Mehra , Aditya Marwaha The Effect of Coconut Oil pulling on Streptococcus mutans Count in Saliva in Comparison with Chlorhexidine Mouthwash. J Contemp Dent Pract. 2016 Jan 1;17(1):38-41.
https://pubmed.ncbi.nlm.nih.gov/27084861/

60) Francesca Ripari, Federica Filippone, Giulia Zumbo, Francesco Covello, Francesca Zara, and Iole Vozza The Role of Coconut Oil in Treating Patients Affected by Plaque-Induced Gingivitis: A Pilot Study
Eur J Dent. 2020 Oct; 14(4): 558-565.
Published online 2020 Sep 22.
https://www.ncbi.nlm.nih.gov/pmc/articles/PMC7535963/

61) C I Ikaraoha, N C Mbadiwe, C J Anyanwu, J Odekhian, C N Nwadike, H C Amah
The Role of Blood Lead, Cadmium, Zinc and Copper in Development and Severity of Acne Vulgaris in a Nigerian Population, Biol Trace Elem Res. 2017 Apr;176(2):251-257. Epub 2016 Sep 6.
https://pubmed.ncbi.nlm.nih.gov/27600928/

Thank you

Printed in Dunstable, United Kingdom